Come Apart

before

You Come

A-P-A-R-T

A HOW-TO GUIDE FOR WOMEN'S RETREATS
Jan Petersen

J&J Publishing

Sugar Hill, GA

Jan Petersen/J&J Publishing
151 Price Hills Trail
Sugar Hill, GA 30518
ComeApart2retreat@gmail.com
www.comeapart2retreat.wix.com/petersen

Book Layout ©2013 BookDesignTemplates.com

Come Apart before You Come A-P-A-R-T/ Jan Petersen —1st Ed.
ISBN 978-0-9908762-5-0

Contents

This book is dedicated to
my sisters at
Community Bible Church
who responded with
grace
as the Lord taught me
about what it means to
"Come Apart".

ACKNOWLEDGEMENTS

Without the enablement of my Lord and Savior, Jesus Christ, this book would not have been written. It is He who planted the idea in my heart to put years of notes and experiences into this form and walked with me through each step of the process.

Without the prayers and support of my husband, John, through the years as retreats were planned and conducted, they would not have happened. Along with him, my sons had to fill some holes left by mom at times. Thanks, Tim, Dan and Jonathan.

Without the careful, needful, and helpful editing eye of Linda, your task as a reader to search out and decipher any material of benefit would be much more difficult.

Without the artistic sense and skill of Janice, you would not have a lovely cover to invite you into the following pages.

Without Rebecca, who the Lord sent along to walk beside me at just the right time, I would still be floundering in the sea of self-publishing.

And without the many retreat planning team members throughout the years who nixed, added to, or modified the initial ideas, the retreats outlined here would be sadly deficient. Among those team members, two stand out as the greatest contributors, both through prayer and with content, DeEtt and Linda.

To each of you go my heartfelt thanks. Without you this manuscript would not be in your hands.

INTRODUCTION

I love retreats! From the time I was a teenager I looked forward to attending them. The very first ladies retreat I attended took place at a local church with ladies from about five other churches, all of the same denomination. We brought sleeping bags and spread out on the linoleum floor, each church group having their own classroom. It obviously wasn't the facilities that brought us! We looked forward to fellowship as sisters in Christ and the time to "come apart." Well, ladies retreats have come a long way since then, and I doubt if today you could get many woman in America to participate under such rustic conditions as those described in my first one!

After attending various ones, I gradually became interested in planning them, an outgrowth of His organizational gifting. Over these last 25 years, God has privileged me to participate in the planning and implementation of a number of retreats. After the retreats were over, the notes, programs and accompanying papers were filed away. So there they sat in file folders. Recently, the Lord planted the thought that perhaps they could be used by others considering the planning of a retreat. Perhaps you have never undertaken such a task and don't know where to start. Or maybe you have planned many, but are looking for some fresh ideas. Outlined in *Come Apart* before You Come A-p-a-r-t are reasons why a retreat is unique from other women's events or activities, considerations in planning one, the components that comprise one plus detailed plans for ten different retreats. The ideas range from a boot camp for training in godliness to a comparison of our hearts to a home, from imagining what God wants for each of us personally to the importance of woman's friendships.

Please use these retreat examples as a springboard from which you design a retreat uniquely suited to your ladies and your situation. Feel free to add to, delete or adapt anything you read in these pages. Above all, seek the Holy Spirit's guidance from the first thought you jot down to the last closing moment of the retreat. As Moses said to God in Exodus 33:15,

> *If Your presence does not go with us, do not lead us up from here.*

Though a retreat can, and should be an enjoyable time for your ladies, you also have the opportunity to make this a significant spiritual experience, and as such, you will encounter spiritual opposition. Therefore, you want, *and need*, Him to lead while you follow. If you approach this challenge with that perspective, you will find it a time of spiritual growth for yourself, as well. Are you ready for some excitement and blessing? Do you want to see God work? Do you want to challenge women to spiritual growth? Let's get started then!

Part I

Retreat "101": How-to's

CHAPTER 1

Retreat Uniqueness

What makes a retreat different from other women's activities? What sets them apart? Is it really worth all the work? These may be some of the questions you have asked yourself in pondering retreats, and they are valid questions. Consider these answers:

- An extended time with the other women in your group provides an opportunity for bonding that rarely happens in a two- or three-hour time period together. "Living together" affords different shared experiences than just "being together" does.

- When you go away for a retreat, you leave behind the demands of home, the distractions of daily life, and your normal routine. Because of that, you can give fuller attention to all that God has to offer during this time.

- New surroundings can awaken your senses and take you from the regular life that often lulls you into a routine, mundane existence to a new awareness of God and fresh experiences in your spiritual life.

- Escaping from the norm offers a chance for refreshment, as well as a renewed and sharpened focus on the life God has given you. We live in a hectic, hurried world where slowing down enough to focus and ponder presents a challenge that often goes unmet. We may feel that everyone wants a piece of us. Or the stresses and difficulties we face make us feel we are living in a "pressure cooker." Or it may just be that we are getting dizzy from the merry-go-round of life that is stuck on a never-ending ride. We begin to think that if something doesn't change, we might come apart.

This is what one frequent retreat participant had to say:

> *I have participated/served in many retreats and cannot express or stress enough how beneficial retreats are. I have learned something at each one about my Lord and myself. I believe the Lord instilled in women to "connect" with one another and the times of prayer and fellowship at retreats have given me some of my most precious memories. To minister and be ministered to by my fellow sisters has been one of the greatest blessings of my Christian life. I am forever grateful for the opportunity retreats have given for this to happen, for on my own I would not have had this blessing. Lori Dorman, retreat participant.*

Jesus recognized the value of "retreats" for His disciples. Scripture records several occasions where they withdrew to a secluded place.

> *And he said unto them, 'Come....apart into a desert place, and rest a while: for there were many coming and going, and they had no leisure so much as to eat.' Mark 6:31 (KJV)*

In the old English of the King James Version, to come apart meant Jesus was inviting them to get away with him for a little while for rest and renewal. So to, I urge you to make plans to Come Apart before You *Come A-P-A-R-T*."

CHAPTER 2

Retreat Considerations

P lanning and conducting a retreat involves a myriad of consid-erations and details. From facilities to food, activities to pub-licity, speaker to servants, each topic is addressed in the following pages. The details given here may seem obvious to those of you who are natural planners and organizers, but others will find the specifics helpful. They are based on past experience, mistakes, and evaluations from planning and conducting retreats, but they are certainly not the only way to go about organizing a retreat. No doubt, many of you have better ideas than those presented here.

BUDGET: Having a budget set at the outset will guide many of your decisions. Will the ladies each pay their own way? Will your church budget pick up part of the costs? Would you like to offer scholarships for those who would otherwise not be able to attend? If so, decide how you would offer them and fund them. (When we were aware of a situation where the cost was likely a factor and thought the individual might not ask for a scholarship, we offered it.) Could a fundraiser offset some of your expenses? Begin with an approximate total amount for which you would like to have as the maximum cost. Then determine how much you will allow for housing, food, speaker, (if applicable), activity costs and miscellaneous items.

FACILITIES: One of the most challenging parts of planning a retreat is the location and type of facility to choose. Depending on the popularity of the facilities, you will need to reserve it six to twelve months out. The type of retreat, the target group, and the desired atmosphere all affect which facilities you reserve. An online search for retreat centers or camps will yield many results. Asking for suggestions from other churches may also be helpful. Here are some questions to consider in the selection process.

- How many women will share a room? Are there bunk beds? Will that be in an issue?
- Are linens included?
- How many women will have to share a bathroom?
- Do we want an informal area for unstructured times?
- How far are we willing to drive to get there?
- Is the cost per room or per individual?
- Is there a kitchen available for use or do we want all meals prepared for us? How is it equipped?
- Is there a separate charge for the kitchen and/or meeting rooms?
- What activities are available on the retreat grounds?
- What time of the year do we want to go? (It is helpful to check school calendars for school holidays, besides being aware of other holidays that may cause conflict.)
- What is the required deposit? Is it refundable?
- When does the facility need the final number of attendees?
- What equipment is available for use? (I.e. DVD player, projector, white board, piano)

<u>FOOD</u>: As you think through how you want to handle your meals and how much of your budget to allow for food, consider:

- Meals on the road to your destination and back
- Whether meals are included in the facility cost
- Whether you have the option of preparing some of your own meals
- Buying take-out for one or more of your meals
- The connection of your meals to some aspect of your retreat goal (For example, at the retreat titled *"Boot Camp, Light,"* described later in this book, we served military MRE's to emphasize the training and discipline involved in being a soldier for Christ.)

If you are on a tight budget, food is an area where you can save substantially. Keep in mind that most women enjoy getting away from the normal routine of meal preparation. Mealtime provides an ideal opportunity for fellowship among your ladies, so consider that in your decisions, too. Lingering over a meal is all part of getting to know one another.

<u>SPEAKER</u>: For the times of teaching during your retreat, you may elect to bring in an outside speaker or use a lady (or ladies) from your church. I have seen positive responses from both approaches.

<u>ACTIVITIES</u>: This is a broad category that can include everything from a skit to going for a walk, from having a campfire to making a craft. The sky is the limit as long as you keep in mind the abilities of the ladies, the space and accommodations available at the facility you have chosen, and how they reflect the overall aim of your weekend. (What an aim is, and how you select one will be discussed later in the book.) As you look through the specific retreat examples in Part II of this book, the plethora of options will become obvious. The

purpose of including activities is to give variety to your retreat, introduce or reinforce the aim and/or teachings, as well as offer opportunities for fun and fellowship.

RETREAT LENGTH: Although retreats have most commonly been held from Friday night through early Sunday afternoon, we have conducted them Friday evening through Saturday evening, as well as Saturday morning through Sunday afternoon. The biggest challenge with having only one night away is whether the facility will allow you to stay into the second day for the Friday to Saturday time frame or how early in the day you can use the facility if you begin on a Saturday. We have found it increasingly difficult for ladies to get away for a whole weekend, which is one of the reasons for considering a shorter retreat. Another reason has been to make it more affordable. The longer retreat has the advantage of deeper bonding and fellowship, and more in-depth coverage of a topic.

PLANNING: After the facility is reserved, and a speaker chosen, (if applicable), start praying for a theme for the retreat and for the preliminary plans. If you have chosen the speaker because of a certain topic she teaches, then that becomes your theme. Otherwise, when you have chosen your theme or topic, pass that on to the speaker, along with your aim, plans for the number and length of teaching sessions, and any other expectations of her for the retreat. Chapter 3 outlines these areas in more detail. About three months, minimum, before the event, schedule the first meeting with a retreat team. The team may be formed from volunteers or prayerful personal selection. The advantages of planning as a team versus one individual are:

- sharing of the responsibilities
- providing balance
- hearing multiple perspectives and ideas

- receiving mutual encouragement
- greater prayer support

A team of two can work, but based on experience, three or four is better. A team larger than this complicates the scheduling of meetings, and may actually be less efficient and effective overall. The team members do not have to make all the preparations. Many tasks can be accomplished by volunteers.

TIMELINE for planning meetings: three months before retreat, two months, and three to four weeks.

First meeting objectives:

1. Determine the theme, aim, and title of the retreat.
2. Select a key verse to tie it together.

(The productivity of the meeting is greatly increased if the team leader comes to the meeting with suggestions in each of these aforementioned components.)

3. After these areas are decided, discuss what the focus of the teaching times will be.
4. Discuss possible activities that will flesh out the aim of your retreat.
5. Assign responsibilities and schedule the next planning meeting for about one month later.

Begin and end each meeting with a prayer time.

> *The mind of man plans his way, but the LORD directs his steps. Proverbs 16:9 .*

Include requests for God's leading and wisdom in selecting the theme and aim for the retreat, creative ideas that support these, unity as a planning team, spiritual protection from the enemy, volunteers to help carry out the preparations and execution of the retreat, joy in service, and for God to begin to prepare the hearts of the ladies who will attend. Mark Batterson coined the word "praystorm" which aptly describes this process.

Don't just brainstorm; praystorm (Batterson, 2012)

Second meeting objectives:
1. Finalize and refine the theme, aim, and title. Select the theme song.
2. Share progress on assignments given out at last meeting and determine if further action is needed.
3. Select from the activities proposed at the last meeting the ones which you want to include.
4. Determine the schedule for the weekend.

Be careful not to plan schedule too tightly. It will take longer than you think to transition from one activity to another and the larger the group, the longer the transition. You don't want the ladies to feel hurried or deprived of time to connect with one another. Part of the reason they came is to relax and have fellowship. Always build some free time into the schedule. (See suggested schedules in Part II for examples in making a schedule.) Also, allow time for the ladies to warm up to each other. Beginning too "deep" or with something that requires them to get very personal gives a forced feeling and a slow start to the retreat. A game, craft or skit are all good ice breakers.

5. Discuss volunteer needs.
6. Delegate responsibilities.
7. Schedule final planning meeting for about one month before retreat.

(In between meetings there will be necessary short communications with team members, as well as with volunteers. These can usually be done via email to keep the planning process moving forward.)

Final meeting objectives:
1. Follow up with each team member on responsibilities given at last meeting.
2. Go through schedule with a fine tooth comb and adjust, as needed.
3. Review which person is responsible for each part of the retreat.

VOLUNTEERS: Besides the planning team, you will need volunteers to help with the details of the retreat. By looking at your schedule, you will be able to determine the tasks for which you could use volunteers. Clear and frequent communication is crucial to assure they understand what needs to be done and the time frame in which it needs to be completed. Let them know that someone will be following-up with them. This step is essential to avoid last-minute scrambling, and to promote a smooth flowing retreat.

PUBLICITY: As soon as you have a date scheduled for your retreat, communicate that to the ladies so they can put it in their calendar. Periodically, remind them of the upcoming retreat with information like the estimated cost, location, title, and a reminder of the dates for the retreat, including registration time frame. Don't give them too many details as you want to build curiosity and interest by "salting the oats." Publicity can include any or all of the following: e-mails, announcements on the church's web site and bulletin, posters, skits and verbal announcements. A graphic designed to coordinate with the retreat theme can be used in all methods of communication to give continuity. Your publicity needs to be presented in multiple forms because no one media method will reach everyone. It also helps keep it fresh in their memory.

REGISTRATION: Conduct registration for a minimum of three weeks, but probably no longer than four to five weeks. Experience has shown that many will wait until the last week to register, no matter how much time is given. Always leave several days margin from when you officially end registration until you turn in the number of attendees to your facility, and others who need a count. Often, someone will call after the deadline wanting to know if they can still attend.

The registration form should reiterate all the crucial information. Include an area at the bottom for registrant to fill in their personal information, detach, and submit, along with a deposit. A deposit gives you working cash for purchases up front as well as making the attendee's commitment firmer. You will need to decide if the deposit is refundable up to a certain date for those who cancel for some reason. The portion of the form they return could also contain a place for them to indicate how they would be willing to volunteer. Keep the form concise, attractive and no longer than one page. Include the name and number of a contact person for any questions your ladies may have.

One to two weeks before the retreat, send each attendee an information sheet with a list of what they need to bring. Be sure to include:

- Attire
- Monies needed
- Bible
- A prepared heart
- Time and place of departure

- Expected time of return
- Any other pertinent information

At the retreat, collect any outstanding balances. This is also a great time to distribute nametags and programs.

BOOKKEEPING: The bookkeeper could also serve as the registrar. This person keeps track of monies spent, the amount received from retreat deposits, and remaining amount received at the time of the retreat. She will also reimburse each person who has made expenditures and assure payment to the facility and speaker.

FINAL CHECKLIST: As you enter the final two weeks before the retreat, go through this checklist to make sure you have taken care of the last minute details.

- Distribute an information sheet to attendees (including speaker, if applicable). This includes everything they need to know to prepare for the retreat: beginning and ending times, meeting location, what to bring, what to wear, and what to expect.
- Give final number of attendees to retreat facility.
- Communicate with the speaker regarding final details.
- Compose a list of supplies or equipment you will need to take. (Don't forget payment to speaker and facility).
- Have directions to destination for each driver.
- Check with each volunteer to make sure responsibilities are completed.

PRAYER: I have already spoken to the need for prayer several times in the previous pages. But prayer cannot be emphasized too much or too often. Without prayer, pride surfaces, the Spirit is quenched, details are forgotten, people become offended, discouragement sets in, and feelings of being overwhelmed take over. Even with prayer these factors are possible, but may go unnoticed or not appropriately handled. A retreat is a lot of work, and without prayer for God's enabling grace, it becomes a lot harder. Without prayer, it is a work of the flesh; with prayer, it is a work of the Spirit. Undertake prayer personally, as a team, and request it from others. Pray before you begin planning, as you are planning, throughout the retreat, and even afterwards.

Commit your works to the LORD and your plans will be established. Proverbs 16:3

CHAPTER 3

Retreat Components

L isted below are the parts that make the whole. Though given and explained separately, they all interrelate.

<u>AIM</u>: What is the goal for this time in which you "come apart?" The aim concisely describes what you hope will occur in the lives of those attending the retreat. Determining an aim provides a common thread which weaves throughout the whole retreat, from your key Scripture verse to your activities to your teachings. It gives your speaker direction. It gives purpose to your time away, increases impact, and unifies everything you do. The examples of specific retreat plans in Part II delineate aims to give you examples for what this is all about.

<u>THEME VERSE AND SONG</u>: The theme verse and song support the aim. Choose a verse that is concise, clearly understood, and easily remembered. Select a song that is either already familiar to some or at least "singable" and easy to learn. Alternately, the theme song can be one that will be used as a special number at several different, appropriate times.

TITLE: Make the title short and catchy, a brief phrase that encapsulates your retreat aim. It can be a question, a play on words, part of the theme verse, or a take-off from some popular cliché. Most often, in my experience, the Lord has given an idea for the theme or topic for a retreat first, and from that we build the framework of an aim, key verse and title.

GROUPS (Large, small, and individual): As the saying goes, "variety is the spice of life." That applies to providing a variety of sizes in groups throughout the retreat, as well. You may have noticed that the dynamics vary greatly between a large group, (more than 12-14) and a small group. Many place the ideal size for a small group at six to eight. The purposes for each sized group also differ. A larger group provides a setting for teaching whereas a small group more easily lends itself to interactive discussion and sharing. Personal time allows opportunity for reflection, meditation, prayer, personal study, and conviction from the Holy Spirit to the individual.

Tips for leading a small discussion groups:

- It is helpful to jot down the desired starting time next to each question so you can pace yourself to get through all the questions. This is meant as a guideline, not to quench the Spirit.
- When there are a number of scripture verses to look up, it saves time to assign all of them at the beginning to different individuals so they can be prepared to read at the appropriate time.
- Encourage everyone to participate, trying to avoid letting the "talkers" dominate. A tip for this challenge is to say, "I'd like to hear from someone I haven't heard from yet", after you give the question. If you have someone who is really

quiet, consider asking them a simple question, being sensitive to the depth of the question in relation to the lady's spiritual maturity. You can also encourage the shyer ones by stating at the outset that everyone's opinions and perspectives are valuable and sought. They have insights, experiences, and perspectives that no one else has.
Always pray for guidance and sensitivity from the Holy Spirit before leading a discussion group.

TEACHING: The number of teaching times scheduled depends on the length of the retreat, the length of each lesson, and the arrangements made with your speaker. In general, two to three sessions seem to work well, but we have had some retreats with four or five "mini" sessions.

ACTIVITIES: Listed below are some the activities we have included in our retreats. When necessary for understanding, particulars on those activities and how they were conducted are included in the detailed plans found in Part II. Always try an activity beforehand, if possible, to alert you to possible obstacles or unexpected consequences. Let your creativity flow balanced by the constraints of time, budget, and facilities.

- Skit
- Game (group, individual, active, pencil and paper, funny, ice-breaker, relationship building)
- Exercise time/walking/hiking
- Communion
- Movie showing
- Campfire
- Foot washing
- Tea Party

- Scavenger Hunt
- Craft (keep simple for the "non-crafty" ladies)
- Writing a letter to God
- Memory verse activity
- Group prayer time

SINGING: As we sing together in worship and praise, God ministers to our hearts in a way that words alone do not. Select songs that relate to your theme, that emphasize your theme and that are, for the most part, familiar to your ladies. Special music by a single lady or small group can also greatly enhance your worship. The songs also prepare hearts for a message, emphasize a truth, or offer the opportunity for personal commitment to the Lord at the conclusion of a lesson.

FELLOWSHIP: Traveling, eating, sharing a room, relaxing, and learning together all provide bonding opportunities. This process naturally occurs as you spend this time together so it is not something extra to fit into your schedule. However, fellowship goes deeper that just chit chat or proximity to one another. The New Testament definition includes community and intimacy.

> But if we walk in the Light, as He Himself is in the light, we have fellowship with one another,... I John 1:7

This usually does not occur during the first hours together, but happens more freely as the retreat progresses. The focus of Biblical fellowship is on what is held in common spiritually and happens as women share what God is doing in their lives, where they are struggling, as they pray together, and as they reach out to minister to one another formally or informally.

My fondest memory is always going with my mom on retreats. Those times will always be special to me....even when separated from my mom, we still had a good time and it forced me to open up to the other women. Michelle Carney, retreat participant.

FREE TIME: It is a balancing act to pack the schedule with lots of meaningful and enjoyable activities and yet leave enough time for the ladies to relax and enjoy "down" time, so make sure to include free time in your schedule. This allows each lady to have some time to choose how she would like to spend it rather than having every minute spelled out. It also builds a little margin into the schedule in case it takes longer than you have allowed for the different activities, (which most certainly will happen at some point during the retreat!). The larger the group, the more margin you need.

Now, for the fun part; examples of actual retreats to get your gears turning and the excitement flowing for the time God wants your group to *Come Apart.* Hopefully, these planning tools will help so that in the process YOU do not "Come A-P-A-R-T". Remember to utilize these ideas just as a starting place so that the retreat becomes your own.

Part II

Retreat "102":
Program Ideas

CHAPTER 4

Who Are You Wearing?

H ave you ever wondered how to develop or better demonstrate humility? How can you model Christ so that He gets the credit instead of you? This "fashionable" retreat will guide you in these endeavors.

Aim: To spotlight God's grace which enables us to embrace a lifestyle of "hiddenness," allowing others to see only Him.

Theme verse: *and all of you clothe yourselves with humility toward one another, for God is opposed the proud but gives grace to the humble.* I Peter 5:5b

Theme song: *Grace Alone* by Jeff Nelson/Scott Wesley Brown

Sample schedule: (This schedule is for the leaders, the participants don't need as many details. Numbers in parenthesis correspond to notes of explanation.)

Friday

5:30 Meet at designated location

Dinner (en route or at retreat location)

7:15 Arrival at retreat location: registration, nametag activity (1), and getting settled

8:00 Welcome and skit (2)

Introduction of retreat aim and theme verse, explain Humble Hannah project (3)

8:15 Movie and popcorn (4)

9:45 Group discussion of movie (4)

10:15 Free time

11:00 Lights out

Saturday

8:30 Continental breakfast

9:30 Personal devotions (use handout composed of scriptures and questions related to upcoming teaching sessions)

10:15 Singing

Teaching session 1 (5)

11:15 Activity: hidden servants (6)

11:30 Free time

12:15 Lunch (7)

1:00 Activities: Invisible names (8) and Hide and Seek (9)

2:30 Singing/Teaching Session 2

3:45 Activities: Invisible man (10), Hidden pins (11)

4:00 Free time

5:15 Invisible names (8) and nametag activities (1)

5:30 Dinner (serve "hidden" foods)

6:15 Wrap-up Session (12): Singing, celebration through sharing, closing song and prayer

7:15 Pack up and departure

Notes:

1. *Nametags*: Find a website which produces word-search puzzles, of which there are many, to create name tags. Make each name tag unique with the name of the intended lady hidden in it, in one place. For the rest of the puzzle use various names of God (Jesus, Savior, Lord, Messiah, etc.) A puzzle made to locate names reading only from left to right and top to bottom, is easier when searching for the hidden names. As each nametag is given to the appropriate lady, she looks for her own name, and only her name, and highlights it. The intent is to represent the fact that when we are living in the flesh, people see us, not Christ. Near the end of the retreat, the ladies then highlight all the names of God, IN THE SAME COLOR in which they had highlighted their own name, symbolizing the desire for people to see Christ when they look at us. It demonstrates that although our essence is present, we are "hiding" in Him.

2. *Skit*: The theme was a runway with models where commentators reviewed what each model was wearing. Three models were negative examples and one was a positive example of women either drawing attention to themselves or to their designer. At the end of this section you will find the script we used.

3. *Humble Hannah project*: A challenge to each lady to look for ways throughout the retreat to serve others in secret (humbly, not to be seen by others). It can be as simple as discretely making someone's bed or going last in the food line.

4. *DVD*: *The Grace Card* (with David G. Evans, Michael Joiner and Mike Higgenbottom, 2010). In order to help them look for specific things as they watch the movie, give some questions before hand.

Discussion questions about movie:

- Who demonstrated humility and how did they show it?
- Who received grace as a result of showing humility? Give the circumstances.
- In what situation did pride stand in the way of receiving grace?
- What did Sam do to finally reach Mac?
- How does forgiveness, whether asking for it or receiving it, show humility?

5. *Teaching sessions*: specific teaching times were on characters in the Bible who, in humility, sought to draw attention to God rather than to themselves.

6. *Hidden Servants*: we chose our pastors as example of servants who humbly undertake many tasks of which few in the congregation are aware. The ladies were asked to share what they thought our pastors were involved in on a day-to-day basis.

7. *Hidden foods*: Prepare foods with hidden ingredients and let the ladies guess what those ingredients are. See www.sneakychef.com for ideas. We served some at lunch and some at dinner.

8. *Invisible names*: Make invisible ink with half lemon juice and half water. Ask the ladies to identify an individual who served as a "hidden person" in their lives. It could be someone in the background of their life that impacted them in quiet ways, maybe prayed for them, influenced them as a child, or authored a book they read that was life-changing, or in some other way blessed them. Using a toothpick or tiny paint brush, write that name on an index card. After several hours, use heat (i.e. embossing gun, hair blower or bare light bulb)

to heat up the paper, thereby revealing the name. Provide an opportunity to share about this person in the wrap-up session.

9. *Hide and Seek*: Print the theme verse on paper in a large font, cut apart, keeping each word on a separate slip, and then hide the slips of paper. (Be sure to keep your own record of where they are hidden or you might have a difficult time remembering.) Have them search for each word and record where it was found, but not remove! To demonstrate humility, the prize was awarded to the one who found the least number of words, rather than the one who found the most. Of course, you don't announce that until the prize is awarded. (Being recognized as #1 may evoke pride, the opposite of the humility we want to encourage.)

10. *Invisible Man*: Show a short video clip (available on YouTube at the time of this writing) of the *Invisible Man*, Lui Boli. (Not the movie by that same title.) Before showing it, ask the question, "If you were going to visually demonstrate humility, what would it look like?" After hearing responses, suggest that this clip could be one way to picture humility. After watching the presentation, ask, "Based on these images what do you learn about humility?"

11. *Hidden pins*: Hide 25 safety pins (the tiny, gold ones) in two cups of rice which are in a gallon sized zip loc bag. Blindfold one person at a time with the instructions to find as many pins she can and remove from the bag in two minutes. (Even though it doesn't seem like it would be, this is VERY difficult to do. The average in our group was to find two pins in the allotted time.) This activity demonstrates that even though we are physically present, (like the pins), we don't want to draw attention to ourselves, but instead, we want others to only be aware of Jesus (represented by the rice).

12. *Share* how God has used a "hidden" person in your life, (identified in the invisible name activity). Also consider and share how God may have been working in your life in hidden ways during this retreat (i.e. through a Humble Hannah, through your personal study, through the teachings, or movie, etc.) End sharing time with restating aim for retreat and the closing song.

Skit script: *Fabulous Frivolous Fashion Show* by Lori Dorman (retreat team member).

Commentator 1 (C1): Welcome, Ladies! How delightful to have you all with us today! We hope you enjoy today's FABULOUS FRIVOLOUS FASHION SHOW!! We know how you "Designer Divas" are going to LOVE this year's line up!

Commentator 2 (C2): Oh, yes! We have everyone, darling! We have Coco Channel and Gucci, Armini, Olga Cassini and soooo many more! Listen closely to catch your favorite designer!

C1: Let's star and you decide...Who are YOU going to be wearing this season?!

(Models enter runway, in turn, carrying placard with label with one hand while using other hand for gestures.)

#1 Judgmental: military march, arm up in a salute, look left, right, up, down, like an inspector, glaring.

C2: First down our runway is that famous designer...Vera WRONG.

C1: Just look at this garment! Why every seam is under scrutiny!

C2: Every button is placed perfectly! While wearing this dress you can put everyone in their place with your perfectionism and knowledge of all that is right!

C1: Yes! You judge her correctly! Rom. 14:10 says, *You then, why do you judge your sister? Or why do you look down on your friend? For we will all stand before God's judgment seat.*

#2 Worry: walk in a "tizzy", weaving around or in circles, pick at imaginary buttons, bows, etc.

C1: Next, we have, uh, well, I think...wait, yes, this is ANNE KLEIN-NOT, from her "I cannot stop worrying line."

C2: Oh my! She is fussing over her dress! Fiddling with the buttons, re-arranging the bows.

C1: Why, she's not put together at all! She's a mess and not wearing her dress well at all! It is "wearing her out."

C2: Ahh...I Peter 5:6,7 says, *Humble yourselves under God's might hand....Cast all your cares upon him.*

#3 Anger: stomps, looks grim/mad, glares, huffs-puffs, one hand on hip.

C2: Wow! Look at this steamin' hot number from Kim MAD-a-sian!!! What a fiery statement this designer makes!

C1: Whew! You can see and smell the smoke! This dress announces itself before it even gets in the room!

C2: You know exactly how searing words and blazing retorts will accessorize this ensemble!

C1: Hope someone has a fire extinguisher!

C1: Here goes! Colossians 3:12, 13 *clothe yourselves with humility, gentleness and patience. Bear with one another and forgive whatever grievances you may have against one another.*

#4 Control: like a robot, no smile, stiff, stilted steps, and arms at side

C2: Alright! Look smart now: No dilly-dallying! Make way for Liz CONTROL-BORNE!

C1: Every strip is lined up! Not a single wrinkle anywhere-they wouldn't dare show up?

C2: Every accessory does its job. No slackers here! This stand alone, multi-tasking, always working outfit does it all. What a reliable and dependable dress! Though it IS beginning to fray around the edges and looks a bit drab.

C1: Oh, who cares? You can wear this outfit anywhere, 24/7 it is ready; this do-it-myself style of the year.

C2: But, um... Psalm 20:7 says, *some trust in chariots and some in horses, but we trust in the name of the Lord our God.*

#5 Pride: walks with nose in the air, walks "grandly" in big sweeping strides. Use free arm to curve over head (think ballerina), then do a "queenly wave" to audience. At end of walk "stumble" as verse is read.

C1: Oh, I am so excited...here it comes – the coveted designer....Gloria Vander-BEST.

C2: Look at this grand, flowing, puffed up dress!

C1: Oooooh... to be elevated to such grandeur. This dress has it all!

C2: And this gal gets noticed! And she knows it!

C1: Proverbs 16:18 says (cue for model to stumble) Pride goes before destruction, a haughty spirit before a fall.

#6 Humility: Walks with small, even steps. Don't shuffle, just quietly and slowly. Don't hang head, but have eyes looking slightly downward, gracious smile on face.
(Both commentators together gasp, looking horrified.)

C1: Oh no! This can't be! A NO-NAME designer has gotten into the lineup!

C2: Look at the simplicity, you hardly notice this garment!

C1: (realization dawning) Yet! Such elegance, such pure lines. Actually ... quite beautiful.

C2: (realization growing) Yes, it seems to draw you to it.

C1: Utterly stunning!

C2: I can't quite put my finger on it, but it appears to reflect a heavenly image!

C1: Absolutely designed to perfection!

C2: I Peter 5:5b *All of you clothe yourselves with humility toward one another, because God opposed the proud, but gives grace to the humble.*

To audience: Who are YOU wearing?

CHAPTER 5

My Lord, My Love

What *is your relationship with Jesus like? How did it start? Where is it going? What is your part in the relationship to make it grow? This retreat will lead you into a deeper love for the Lord Jesus Christ, the One who loves you like no other.*

<u>Aim</u>: to gain a deeper understanding of God's unconditional love for me, which leads me to a deeper love for Him and others.

<u>Theme verse</u>: *We love, because He first loved us.* I John 4:19

<u>Theme song</u>: *Knowing You* by Graham Kendrick

<u>Sample schedule</u>: (This schedule is for the leaders, the participants don't need as many details. Numbers in parenthesis correspond to notes of explanation.)

(Place a vase containing a single silk rose along with a letter printed on pretty stationary, in each woman's room beforehand. Write the letter, identical for each woman except for the name to whom it was addressed, as if it was a love letter from God to her.)

Saturday
9:00 Departure
11:30 Lunch at a restaurant
1:00 Arrive at destination
1:45 Craft project (1)
3:00 Singing
Teaching Session 1: _My First Love_ (2)
4:00 Communion and prayer time: prayers of praise (who God is) and thanksgiving (what God has done)
5:00 Free time
6:00 Supper
7:30 Singing
Teaching Session 2: _How Can I Show God I Love Him?_ (3)
9:00 Snacks, fellowship, and free time

Sunday
8:00 Fruit, coffee, and tea available
8:30 Group prayer time
9:00 Personal quiet time: write a love letter to the Lord
9:45 Free time
10:30 Brunch
11:30 Singing
Teaching Session 3: _Loving Others, Including those 'Sandpaper People'_ (4)
12:30 Small group discussion (based on previous teaching session)
1:15 Sharing time: closing comments (restate Aim) and prayer
2:00 Pack up and departure

Notes:

1. *Craft project:* Treasure Box. As a reminder of how God treasures us, make treasure boxes in which small items that we treasure can be placed. We decoupaged cigar boxes, but any small paper mache or wooden box would work. If wooden boxes that need to be sanded are used, a tie-in to the idea of "sandpaper people" could be made in the third teaching session.

2. *Teaching Session 1: My First Love* Romans 5:5-8
Resource used: *Knowing God* by J. I. Packer

3. *Teaching Session 2: How Can I Show God I Love Him?*
I. Types of Hearts. Description of hearts as found in the Bible: clean, pure, wise, and contrite, (along with contrasting types of heart)
II. Demonstrating Love: Find ways to remind ourselves of Jesus throughout day.
Examples:
- Treasure what He says to you
- Delight in His gifts to you
- Choose things that please Him
- Use creative ways to express love to Him
- Love those He loves

4. *Teaching Session 3: Loving Others, including those 'Sandpaper People'*
Resource used: *Irregular People* by Joyce Landorf

Suggested changes: Allow longer or more opportunities for free time than this schedule allows.

CHAPTER 6

Boot Camp, Light

I n what areas of life do you work hard? Do you expend great effort and discipline in those areas that are not important to you? Would you if you found out there would be a valuable payoff if you did? This 'military-flavored' retreat explores that perspective on a spiritual level while incorporating physical training activities.

Aim: to understand that our training in godliness, which requires effort and discipline, is of great value and benefit.

Theme verse...*Train yourself to be godly. For physical training is of some value, but godliness has value for all things, holding promise for both the present life and the life to come.* I Timothy 4:7b, 8 NIV

Theme song: *More Like You* by Scott Wesley Brown.

Sample schedule: (This schedule is for the leaders, the participants don't need as many details. Numbers in parenthesis correspond to notes of explanation.)

Saturday

0800 Report for active duty, load transport vehicles

0815 Roll call, induction and marching orders (instructions) (1)

0830 Troops deployed to _____ (retreat location)

1100 Arrival at _____ (Unpack and settle into barracks, read training manual guidelines)

1130 Marching led by drill sergeant (2)

1200 Chow with meal inspection and awards (3) (Practice memory verse together at each meal.)

1245 Troop meeting (everyone): *Introduction and Training Basics* (4)

1315 Recruit study time (5)

1400-1445 Patrol meetings (6)

1500 Drills (7)

1530 Troop meeting: *Training in Obedience*

1600 Off-duty

1800 Chow with meal inspections and awards (3)

1900 Troop meeting: *Training in Meditation*

1945 War games (8)

2045 Off-duty/rations (snacks)

2200 In barracks (play recording of Taps outside of bedrooms at lights out)

Sunday

0800 Rise and shine: (play recording of Reveille)

0815 P.T. (exercise time)

0845 Showers

0915 - 1045 Solitary confinement (9)

1100 Chow with meal inspections and awards

1200 Troop meeting: *Training in Prayer and Fasting*

1230 Troop prayer meeting

1315 Pack up and load transport vehicles

1345 Debrief (10)

1500 Departure

1800 Troops discharged to home base

Notes:

1. *Roll Call, Induction, and Marching Orders.* Each recruit receives a Basic Training Manual (Use camouflage paper for the cover and distribute to each recruit during roll call time. In it, place guidelines for the retreat, the schedule, (in military time), theme song, and worksheets for individual study time. The label on the cover gives the name of recruit, her room assignment and the patrol in which she has been placed. Use military names for the patrol names: Alpha, Beta, Charlie, etc., and put five to seven women in a patrol.)

Nametags: Give out at time of roll call and induction. Make them to resemble "military dog tags" with name given as: Recruit _____ (their last name).

Uniform: Camouflage baseball caps, t-shirts, jeans, sweats, and sneakers. (No "designer" exercise ware.) Jewelry limited to watches and wedding rings. Give each woman a "camo" hat as they register. (Remember to communicate the uniform guidelines prior to the retreat.)

The Drill Sergeant's responsibilities are to keep things moving in a timely manner from one activity to another, (whistle optional) conduct inspections, and lead march time.

2. *March*: March around the grounds in formation using one of the familiar march cadences found on YouTube, substituting words included below.

Leader calls out phrase, Recruits, "call back."

Cadence:

I don't know but I believe (recruits repeat each line)
God is always here with me.
Fo-cus
On God
God-li-ness is - (pause for echo) FOR ME!

I'm a soldier in train-ing
Holy Spirit motivate me (motivate in 2 beats)
Fo-cus
On God
God-li-ness is - (pause for echo) FOR ME!

Struggling with forgetfulness
Keeping God first is my test
Fo-cus
On God
God-li-ness is - (pause for echo) FOR ME!

Savior help train me to see
Daily I need time with thee
Prac-tice
For God
God-li-ness is - (pause for echo) FOR ME!

(Written by Lori Dorman, retreat team member)

3. *Chow*: Serve meals in metal pie pans. Everyone cleans up their own "plate", cup and silverware after meals. For one meal we served MRE's which they prepared themselves. (MRE's refer to Military Ready to Eat meals which are packaged meals used by the military when they are out in the field. Everything that is needed for the

meal is in the pouch: utensils drink mix, even the method to heat the entree. They can be purchased on eBay. Retail camping stores also sell survival meals, but are much higher in cost.) At each table, place an officer's hat, (real or faux), at an empty place as a reminder that our "Commanding Officer" is present with us everywhere and at all times. We encouraged the ladies to fast Sunday morning until our first meal at 1100. Food was available in the kitchen for those who did not fast, for whatever reason.

Meal Inspections with Awards (pins on baseball cap) for:

- Saying the memory verse
- Participating in PT
- Passing meal inspections (hat and name tag on, Bible and training manual with them, and proper "uniform")
- Maintaining quiet during Solitary Confinement
- Completing Boot Camp

4. *Introduction*: Our focus this weekend is our devotion to God. We are defining godliness as a devotion to God which results in a life pleasing to Him. (Bridges, The Practice of Godliness, 1983, p. 24ff) In contrast:

> "Ungodliness may be defined as living one's everyday life with little or no thought of God, or of God's will, or of God's glory, or one's dependence on God." (Bridges, Respectable Sins, 2007, p. 54)

This devotion comes from a balance of our fear of God, our understanding of the love of God, and our desire for God.

(Show diagram of a triangle with each element at one point)

I. Fear of God: deep reverence for who God is and holy dread of displeasing Him.

II. Love of God: the more we understand what God's love means to us and what it cost Him, the greater our love for Him will grow.

III. Desire for God: that deep longing for fellowship and intimacy

All of our activities this weekend are to help train us in godliness. Our goal is that you will understand that your training is of great value and benefit. This growth in devotion is evidenced in obedience, in meditation on God's word, in fellowship with Him through quiet time, in prayer, and in worship." During our time together, you will receive training in each of these areas.

1. Training basics includes personal responsibility, commitment, utilizing a coach, and setting goals for growth.

2. Training in obedience comes as a result of developing a fear of God and love for God in response to His love for us.

3. Training in meditation uses scripture to develop godliness, and goes beyond Bible reading.

4. Each of us will have a time of "solitary confinement" to focus on the discipline of spending time alone with God in fellowship.

5. Our training in worship will come through the personal and corporate worship times interspersed throughout Boot Camp.

Conclude the introduction by reading excerpts from Elizabeth Elliot's comments about being *Under Orders* to (Elliot, 1982, p. 24ff).

5. *Recruit study time* (personal study time, first day)

Each recruit has a worksheet in the training manual with these instructions:

- Begin with prayer; asking the Lord to open your heart to receive what He has for you, give you new insights, reveal specific areas of ungodliness, and focus on Him this weekend.
- Now open the letter that is sealed in the envelope you received and read it thoughtfully. (See letter following.)
- What is your reaction to the letter?
- Jerry Bridges defines ungodliness as...

...living ones' everyday life with little or no thought of God, or of God's will, or of God's glory or of one's dependence on God. (Bridges, Respectable Sins, 2007)

- After reading this letter, can you identify areas in your life in which you are giving little or no thought to God? Name them.
- Confess those to God right now and ask Him to strengthen you in this training process of godliness.
- Thinking about the elements of training basics discussed in the troop meeting we just had, in what areas do you struggle, and why do you think that is?
- Look up the following verses and write down a key thought about godliness found in each one.
  I Timothy 4:7
  I Timothy 4:8
  I Timothy 6:6
  Titus 2:11, 12
  II Peter 1:3
- Now read through the memory verse several times, found in your Basic Training Manual. Then write it out to help you begin to memorize it.

(Letter to be read at beginning of Recruit study time)

To my dearest friend,

It will be so good to see you again when you get back into town from your extended vacation. I know it has been a long time since we had time together. It hasn't been intentional; I have just been so busy.

Did I tell you about my latest experience? It was so awesome. I'll try to remember to show you some pictures so you get a better idea of that it was like. It is one of the most exciting things I've ever been involved in. I know I should have waited to do it until you got back so we could do it together, but the sign-up deadline was coming so quickly I just went ahead. It is an expensive hobby, but it's my money, after all.

Things at home have been pretty rough lately with the kids. I know I should have talked to you earlier about Sissy specifically, but I found some good books at the library a friend told me about. "Dear Abby "has some helpful advice, too, sometimes. Next time we talk, I'll tell you more about it. You might even have some wisdom to share with me.

I'm going to be starting a new job next month. It was kind of a quick decision, but everybody I talked to thought it was a good opportunity for me. My husband was quite disappointed I didn't ask his opinion but it all happened so fast I really didn't have time to think about it. It just feels right so I'm sure it will work out.

It has been awhile since I have been to Bible study. With running the kids around, and trying to get all my errands done, and keeping the house up, there's not much time left. Besides, the others in the group all seem so close to God I don't really feel comfortable. Maybe it would help if I read the Bible more often. I'll do that soon.

I've found a great new fiction series at the library. I stay up way too late reading! I've already finished the fifth one in the last month.

One last thing, I saw the doctor again last week because my back problems haven't gotten any better. He thinks I should consider surgery. I'm not really sure what to do. Well, he's the doctor, so I guess I'll do what he thinks is best.

Love,
Your friend

If this letter was actually written by you to God, would anything be true to your life? Where you see ungodliness as defined by Bridges?

6. *Patrol Meeting*: (small group discussion according to designation: Alpha, Beta, etc.) (See tips for leading a small group in Chapter 3.) Questions:

- Do you agree or disagree that ungodliness is the root of all other sin?

- Read together Genesis 5:21-24 and Hebrews 11:5. How do they describe a godly man?
- If we define godliness as devotion to God which results in a life that is pleasing to Him, how is that different from what you thought godliness was?
- Read James 4:13-15. For what expression of ungodliness did James, through the Holy Spirit, condemn those people?

As stated in the introduction, Jerry Bridges identifies three essential elements that comprise godliness, a devotion to God: fear of God, love of God, and desire for God. Let's explore each one briefly.

- What importance do you think there is in having a fear of God, based on I Peter 1:17-19 and Hebrews 12:28, 29.
- What effect should the love of God have on us? See II Corinthians 5:14-15 and I Timothy 1:14-16.
- How do these verses describe a desire for God? Psalm 27:4, Psalm 63:1, Philippians 3:10
- (Optional, if time allows) Is there anything else you learned about godliness from the verses you looked up during recruit study time? (#5)

7. *Drills*: part of training includes being prepared for "battle". Here are several drills you could use.

Group drill:

- Bible sword drill (give a Bible reference to see who can find first)

Each patrol rotates through three stations for the following drills:

Patrol drills:

- Memory verse drill (Write out memory verse ahead of time, one word per slip of paper. Recruits practice putting words in order.)

- Military term match drill (Match military terms to definition)
- Target practice (We used air soft guns with targets.)

8. *War Games*:

- No Smiles Allowed: Have women come one at a time to sit in a chair facing the group. Time how long they can go without smiling. Those in the group can do anything they wish, (as long as they do not touch her), to try to make her crack a smile.
- Military Term Analogy Game: Use the same military terms that were used for the military term match drill earlier, and ask for ladies to share a spiritual analogy that could correspond to the term. Example: *Interdiction*: to attack and disrupt enemy supply lines. Analogy: In our devotion to God we need to recognize and take action to ward off and destroy Satan's schemes.

9. *Solitary Confinement*: (each recruit has this handout in their training manual)
As we continue our training in godliness, you have the opportunity to have an extended time alone with your Lord. He longs to have this uninterrupted time with you. The more you practice spending with Him, the more you will find your desire for Him deepens.

- Start with a time of worship and praise by singing (or saying) the words to our Theme Song, *More Like You* and meditating on what He is like.
- Spend a few minutes in prayer to ask Him to quiet your heart, cleanse your heart, and give you an openness to hear Him speak through His Spirit and His Word.

- Now take some time to "chew and ruminate" on our memory verse to get more food value out of it.
- Read I Timothy 4:6-8:
    1. What commands do you see?

    Reject what?

    Accept what?

    2. How do you think godless myths and old wives' tales apply to us?
    3. Who does the training?
    4. What will training involve for you? (See also II Timothy 2:3-5)
    5. Of the five practices in which we demonstrate godliness, where do you feel you need the most training? (prayer, meditation on Scripture, worship, fellowship with Him in a personal quiet time, or obedience).
    6. What might you need to give up for your training to be more effective?
    7. What is the difference between physical training and spiritual training?
    8. What do you consider to be profitable or of value in life?
    9. How is godliness profitable or valuable? (It might be helpful to also consider the verses you looked up yesterday in your individual study.)
    10. Besides godliness, what else does God consider profitable? II Timothy 3:16, Titus 3:8

- Rewrite I Timothy 4:7b, 8 in your own words.
- How do these verses challenge you? (You will have the opportunity to share this during our debriefing time.)

- Read through the theme verse slowly several times, each time emphasizing a different word.
- Close this time of study by writing a letter to the Lord, your Commanding Officer, with any praises, thanksgivings, requests, or commitments you have made as a result of what He has shown you this weekend.
- If you have any time left, begin reading through Psalm 119. This Psalm beautifully describes the heart of a godly person.

10. *Debrief:*

Awards: Present any awards not yet given for accomplishments.

Prayer followed by the songs:

Turn Your Eyes upon Jesus and the theme song.

Sharing time: (possible topics or questions)

- What aspect of our physical training activities had an impact as it applies to your spiritual training?
- Share one thing you have learned this weekend.
- What conviction has the Holy Spirit put on your heart regarding your training in godliness that you can share with us?

Closing comments: The mark of a godly person is to bring glory to God. This is the goal in training in godliness. (Share illustration of Korean gymnasts: vision implanted and impressed in their minds from very young that any success would be for the glory of their Chairman, and to receive the smile of his approval.)

Whether, then, you eat or drink or whatever you do, do all for the glory of God. I Corinthians 10:31

So how do I bring Him glory? (ask for responses)

- Desire all that I do to be pleasing to Him.

- Determine that all my activities honor Him.
- Defer credit to Him.

Restate aim: When we bring Him glory we are putting the spotlight on Him instead of ourselves. Our Boot Camp "Light" shines when we understand that our training in godliness is of great value and benefit not just for ourselves, but ultimately for His glory.

(Read the following verses in unison and then listen to the words of the song, Holy, Holy, Holy, (Lord God Almighty...) verses 1, 2, and 4. As the song plays, invite ladies to put their "crowns" (hats with awards attached) next to the officer's hat, symbolizing that God, our Commanding Officer, deserves all the glory.

And the four living creatures, each one of them having six wings, are full of eyes around and within; and day and night they do not cease to say, "HOLY, HOLY, HOLY is THE LORD GOD, THE ALMIGHTY, WHO WAS AND WHO IS AND WHO IS TO COME." And when the living creatures give glory and honor and thanks to Him who sits on the throne, to Him who lives forever and ever, the twenty-four elders will fall down before Him who sits on the throne, and will worship Him who lives forever and ever, and will cast their crowns before the throne, saying, "Worthy are You, our Lord and our God, to receive glory and honor and power; for You created all things, and because of Your will they existed, and were created. Revelation 4:8-11

Closing Prayer

Suggested change: Allow more time for discussion (Patrol meeting).

CHAPTER 7

Vessels for the Master

A re you becoming more Christ-like each year? What part do we play in that process and what part does God play? This retreat explores how we can become for useful for the Master's work.

Aim: to understand that as holy vessels we are set apart by God to be used by Him to bring Him glory and honor.

Theme verse: *Therefore, if anyone cleanses himself from these things, he will be a vessel for honor, sanctified, useful to the Master, prepared for every good work.. II Timothy 2:21*

Theme song: *Refiner's Fire* by Brian Doerksen

Sample schedule: (This schedule is for the leaders, the participants don't need as many details. Numbers in parenthesis correspond to notes of explanation.)

Saturday
9:00 Departure
11:00 Shopping along the way
12:30 Lunch at restaurant
1:30 Arrive at destination/unpack/registration
2:30 "Ice breaker" game
3:30 Personal study
4:00 Singing
Session 1: *Vessels that are Set Apart*
5:00 Free time
6:00 Supper
7:30 Singing
Session 2: *Vessels that Bring Honor*
Small group discussion
9:00 Snacks and fellowship

Sunday
8:00 Fresh fruit/coffee/tea available
8:30 Group prayer time (optional)
9:00 Go for a walk (optional)
10:00 Brunch
11:00 Session 3: *Vessels that are Cleansed*
1:00 Communion, singing and sharing
Restate aim: As holy vessels we are set apart by God to be used by Him to bring Him glory and honor.
2:00 Pack up/departure

This retreat was held many years ago, so the details are few and the memories faint, but you have a skeleton which you can flesh out. One memory is of using various types of pitchers as an object lesson representing the different types of vessels to which the theme verse refers. (Some versions use the word instruments instead of vessels.) We displayed a variety, from plastic to crystal. The teaching sessions focused on understanding the doctrine of sanctification, explaining both progressive sanctification, (our growth in holiness) and positional sanctification, (our standing from God's perspective as being already holy because of Christ's finished work on the cross).

Suggestion: A poem entitled, *The Touch of the Master's Hand*, can be found online. The poem is also the basis for a song by the same name as well as a short video. It tells the story of a plain, ordinary violin being auctioned with small, infrequent responses as the bidding begins. But then a master violinist takes the violin from the auctioneer's hands. The violin suddenly "sings" and instantly it becomes an instrument of great beauty, value, and longing. The bidding changes dramatically, depicting the change in how the violin is now viewed.

CHAPTER 8

Beyond Imagining

Y our ladies will enjoy activities and games that spark their im-
aginations. These will help prepare them for studying the
unimaginable riches God has planned for His children, which
He reveals as the depths of His Word are mined. Lots of delightful experiences, and even some surprises, are in store throughout the weekend.
Are you ready to let God take your thinking "outside the box?"

Aim: to learn how to more deeply study God's Word so that we
discover the unimaginable riches which are beyond our wildest
dreams.

Theme verse: *No eye has seen, no ear has heard, and no mind has imagined what God has prepared for those who love him. I Corinthians 2:9*
NLT

Theme song: *Ancient Words* by Lynn DeShazo

Sample schedule: (This schedule is for the leaders, the participants don't need as many details. Numbers in parenthesis correspond to notes of explanation.)

Friday
7:00 Registration and getting settled
8:00 Activity: *You'll Never Guess What I Saw!* (1)
9:00 Skit: *Beyond Imagining* (2)
9:30 Snacks
11:00 Lights out

Saturday
8:00 Breakfast
8:45 Prayer time (optional)
9:15 Quiet time
10:00 Singing
Session 1: *I Never Imagined* (treasures in God's Word for me to discover, 3 question Bible study method explained) (3)
11:00 Stretch break
11:15 Small group discussions
12:00 Free time
12:30 Lunch
1:30 Free time: *Imagine what you could do!*
4:15 Singing
Session 2: *Journey toward the Unimaginable* (3 question method demonstrated and practiced as group with teacher leading through the process.)
5:30 Evaluating your journey
6:00 Free time
6:30 Supper
7:30 Craft: Snow globes: *Let your imagination go!*

8:30 Games: *Imagine that!* (4)
9:30 Campfire and S 'mores
11:00 Lights out

Sunday
8:30 Breakfast
9:15 Quiet time: (suggest scripture passage to practice the *Three Question Study Method)*
10:00 Worship and sharing (based on insights discovered during Quiet time) Restate aim (this one is slightly modified from what is stated at the beginning): We have spent learning to dig deeper into God's Word but we haven't even begun to imagine the fullness of what God wants to reveal to us.
11:30 Pack up
12:00 Lunch
1:30 Departure

Notes:

1. *Activity:* For a fun activity, use the *Magic Eye* picture books to let the ladies see things they would not have imagined are present at first glance.

2. *Skit: Beyond Imagining*

Scene opens with a servant reading a letter aloud:
"As I am currently out of the country, it will be necessary for me to communicate with all my servants through personal representatives, letters, or emails. These communiqués are sent to give you instruction, encouragement, and, as necessary, correction and warnings."
Your King

Servant (S): "Hmm... I wonder what that all means. I already know what my job is, and I am doing fine. Can't be that much that I don't know. Well, speaking of my job, I better get back to it." (Resumes tidying up room)

Narrator (N): As the Narrator says, "Time passes" someone holding a sign with the word "Time" walks across room.

Mailman knocks at the door.

S: Hello

Mailman: "I have a registered letter addressed to Miss Servant of the King."

S: "Yes, that's me! I wonder who is sending me a registered letter. Thank you. Good bye."

(Talking to herself) "The return address says, 'Your King'. I guess I should read it, but I can't imagine there is anything in it I need to know."

(Phone rings and servant goes to answer it, tossing down the letter as she goes to the phone.)

"I've got to answer that. You never know who it could be." (Servant talks on phone for several minutes, inaudible to audience.)

"Back to work, I'll read the letter later. I've got more work than I can handle. Doesn't the King know that this is too much for me to manage alone? Why doesn't he provide someone to help me?"

N: Time passes. (Use sign again.)

S: "I haven't checked my email today. Guess I better take a few minutes and see if there are any important ones."

N: (Voice in background: "You've got mail")

S: "Oh, four messages. Let's see what they're about."
(Reading aloud) "You may be able to get a new lower interest mortgage if you meet our simple qualifications. Reply now to see how we can help you put more dollars in your pocket every month. Just junk. Delete."

"30 days to a younger you". Try our supplement free and see how energetic you will feel in no time. Hmm. Maybe I should order some of that."

"Oh, here's a note from Mom. She's coming for a visit this weekend. Oh, no! I've got tons to do before she comes. I've gotta go right now! I'll read that fourth email later. I see it is from the King. Doesn't he know I have more important things to do than read emails?"

(Servant begins dusting furniture, knocks valuable vase off table, breaking)

"OH, NO!! That was a gift from the King of Priam. I'll never have the money to replace it. (goes on fretting and muttering several minutes) Maybe if I just replace it with another one, the King won't remember what was there."

N: Time passes (Use sign.)

(Phone rings. Servant looks at it as she is sprawled out on the couch and groans, too tired to answer it.)

S: "Not again! That is about the tenth call today! I am just too tired to answer it. It can just go to my voice mail. Nobody appreciates how much work I do around here, especially the King. If he did, he would let me know."(Servant falls asleep.)

N: "Next morning."

(Servant still asleep. Suddenly she wakes with a start, hearing noises and voices outside. She rolls over and peeks out window. A car is going down the road with a bullhorn broadcasting a message).

S: "What's all that noise outside? Don't they know what time it is? Can't I sleep in peace?" (Servant puts pillow over her head, rolls over, and goes back to sleep.)

N: "Next morning."

S: (Servant says while getting up) "I feel terrible, (moans), my head hurts, I ache all over and I feel nauseous. I can't go to work today. I wonder if it could be something I ate yesterday."

N: "Next morning."

S: "Well, I have a lot to do today after missing work yesterday. I better get busy." (Gets broom and starts sweeping. After several minutes there is a knock at the door.)

(Sighing) "What timing! I've just gotten started on my work and somebody wants to visit. Well, I don't have time for a visit today. Some people have to work. (Knock again) If I ignore it, maybe they'll get the hint. (Keeps sweeping, then looks out the window.) Good, they're leaving."

N: "Later that day."

S: "What a day! I'm beat. I'm going to relax this evening. I haven't read my mail, or email, or checked my voice mail for five days. This will be a good chance to do that. I'll start with the letter." (She opens letter and reads aloud).

Dear Miss Servant,
I have received my daily reports from my superintendents and they have reported that some of my servants have too much work for them to handle. You are one of those identified. Because I never want your burden to be greater than you can bear I will be providing a helper. To receive your helper immediately, call the number provided at the bottom of this letter.
Sincerely, The King

(Silence while thinking and staring at the letter.)

"If I had only read the King's letter when it came, I would have gotten help right away instead of struggling all week by myself."(Getting up and going to computer)
"From now on I am going to read my letters every day. (Short pause) I wonder how many emails are unread. Oh, here's that one from the king that I got last week. I'll start with that one." (Servant reads aloud)

Dear Miss Servant,

It has come to my attention that you have been very diligent in your work. It is also reported that you are thorough in each task and trustworthy even when your supervisor is not watching. I want you to know how much I appreciate your work for the kingdom, and remind you of the reward that you will be receiving.

Gratefully, The King

"My efforts are noticed! The King does know! That made my day, what an encouragement. I really could have used that the other day when I was so discouraged. (Short silence) I wonder what I missed by not answering the phone the other day. Oh, and I forgot all about listening to my voice mail."(Servant picks ups phone and retrieves voice mail.)

N: "Hello, Miss Servant. This is the King speaking. I know today is your scheduled day to vacuuming the palace and I forgot to give you this message before I left. The vase that I received from the King of Priam is very fragile and irreplaceable. Therefore, we will have a specialist in cleaning this type of porcelain come to teach you how to care for it. Goodbye."

(Hangs up phone thoughtfully)

S: "My life would sure go better if I took the time to listen to the King."

(Servant opens the door and looks outside, sees a letter on ground outside door, picks it up, and sits down again with letter in hand. Also picks up newspaper and opens it, letter still in lap. Scans newspaper headlines)

"This is interesting. It appears there was a parade yesterday. No... it wasn't a parade. Wait! That looks like the same car that went down my street yesterday making all the noise with the bullhorn. Let me see what it says about it. (Reading from paper) Yesterday, we received an anonymous tip that the city water supply may have been tainted by terrorists. The King has ordered all the citizens to be notified as quickly as possible. The message was broadcast on each street that no one should drink their water unless it is first boiled. Failure to do so could result in such symptoms as headaches, body aches, and nausea." (Puts down newspaper, incredulous)

"The King tried to warn me and I was more interested in sleeping than listening to Him."

(Servant sits in silence a few minutes)

"I never imagined! My opinion of the King is changing. I didn't realize how much he cares about me. He wants to help me, encourage me, teach me, and warn me. I have been ignoring Him when I could have gained so much. Now I will look forward to getting his letters, calls, and emails because they are especially for me. I bet this notice I found outside my door is from him. I can't wait to read it."
(She quickly rips it open and reads aloud.)

To all my servants:
There will be a meeting at 4:00 on _____ for all of my servants. I am offering an opportunity for any of you to receive your freedom, but you must be present to accept my offer. This offer will not be available indefinitely. If you accept this offer your future is 'beyond imagining'.
The King

3. *Three-Question Bible Study Method**

This method can be used whether you have 10 minutes or 10 hours! Determine the amount of scripture you will cover based on the amount of time you have. (Each woman was given a 5 ½" X 8 ½" notebook for this purpose in which the explanation of the study method was put on the inside cover using a half-page label.)

Begin by praying and asking the Holy Spirit to lead your study and open your spiritual eyes and ears so He can teach you what you need to learn through the passage you are about to study. Read the passage. Write down your responses to the following three questions.

1. *What are the core facts in this passage?*
Who? What? When? Where? Why? How? (All of these may not be answered in each passage.) Write down the answers to these questions or a brief summary of the facts of the passage.

2. *What are the life lessons or truths I can learn from this passage?*
Look for a warning, a command, or a promise.
Is there an example to follow or not to follow?
What is the main truth or principle of the passage?
What does the passage reveal about the character of God? (His attributes, ways of relating to people, emotions, views about something, reasons to love Him more, etc.)
(Not all of the above examples will be in every passage. These are only suggestions to help you get started.)

3. *What are some questions that will help me apply these lessons?*
Look back at what you wrote in the first two sections. Write down any application questions that help you apply this lesson to your life.

Avoid using yes or no questions unless you have a follow-up question. Write down your response to the questions.

*Based on a method taught by Bible Study Fellowship International, adapted, modified, and shared by Ronda Gazelle to with the ladies at our retreat.

Example of the 3 Question Bible Study Method (as explained above)

> This is My commandment, that you love one another, just as I have loved you. Greater love has no one than this, that one lay down his life for his friends. You are My friends if you do what I command you. No longer do I call you slaves, for the slave does not know what his master is doing; but I have called you friends, for all things that I have heard from My Father I have made known to you. You did not choose Me but I chose you, and appointed you that you would go and bear fruit, and that your fruit would remain, so that whatever you ask of the Father in My name He may give to you. This I command you, that you love one another. John 15:12-17

- *What are the core facts in this passage?*

Jesus calls his disciples friends, and tells them to love one another, describing what that entails. (The summary form was used vs. Who, What, etc. in this example. Narratives work best for the 5 W's. The summary form is usually easier for instructive passages.)

- *What are the life lessons or truths I can learn from this passage?*

Command: love one another, stated two times

Promise: answered prayer

Example to follow: the way Jesus loved his disciples is the way we are to love

Greatest example of love is to "lay down your life" for a friend

God's purpose for us is to produce enduring fruit.

What I learn about Jesus: Son of God, loving, sovereign, giving.

We are friends of Jesus because He chose us; He initiates a relationship with us.

Jesus calls us His friends if we obey Him.

Jesus revealed the Father.

We pray to the Father on the authority and because of our relationship with Jesus.

- *What are some application questions that will help me apply these lessons?*

What kind of friend am I?

How could I be a better friend?

In what ways is my love for others lacking?

How do we "lay down our lives" for others?

What is the quality of fruit am I bearing? Is it sparse or abundant fruit?

Do I have a relationship with Jesus that gives me authority to pray? How do I know?

What answers to prayer have I recently seen?

4. *Games:*

- *"Can you imagine what I have in my hand?"* We had a collection of unusual objects which were kept hidden, one per lady. One at a time, each woman came and sat in a chair facing the rest of the group. An object was held up, over and behind her head, so she could not see it. She then asked yes or no questions (think 20 Questions game) to try to determine the object. These objects were random, yet common, kitchen or household items, (examples: roll of toilet paper roll, light bulb, disposable diaper).
- *"Can you imagine how this would be used?"* This is a group guessing game. An object is shown for which the ladies try

to guess what it is and how it is used. Again, select random items, but unusual ones that are very unique or rarely used today. Think: things your mother or grandmother used or a tool your husband uses, (examples: sock darner, potato ricer).

We learned the "3-step Bible Study" -- what a "maturing skill" that was for me. I had always relied on "book devotionals" or other "pre-printed" studies...but now, I could take any scripture anytime, anyplace and reap new jewels of God speaking to me. I still use this from time to time (in between our ladies Bible studies or personal books I am reading)! Lori Dorman, retreat participant.

CHAPTER 9

Faith, Friends, and Fun

W hat do like to do with your girlfriends? What purposes do your friendships serve? As you have fun this weekend with girlfriends, be they long-time or new acquaintances, you will explore what God says about the friend – faith connection. Girlfriends are a gift from God that He can use to enrich and change our lives.

Aim: to learn that our friendships with other women are to be reflections of Christ.

Theme verse: A friend loves at all times...Proverbs 17:17b

Theme song: The Servant Song by Richard Gillard

Sample schedule: (This schedule is for the leaders, the participants don't need as many details. Numbers in parenthesis correspond to notes of explanation.)

Friday
3:30 Meet at specified location
4:00 Departure (supper en route to retreat location)
7:00 Arrival at retreat location, settle in
8:00 Get acquainted time, introduction to weekend
8:45 Fun and laughs (We told jokes and funny stories, then watched an *I Love Lucy* DVD.)
10:00 Free time and snacks
11:00 Lights out

Saturday
8:30 Breakfast
9:00 Personal devotions (1)
9:30 Group prayer time, optional
10:00 Craft project (Suggestion: make hats or decorate pre-made hats to wear to the tea party scheduled later in the day.)
10:45 Singing
Session 1: Friendship Defined (2)
11:30 Discussion groups: (questions based on previous teaching session)
12:15 Free time
1:00 Lunch
2:00 Free time
4:00 Tea party
5:00 Singing
Session 2: Friendship Demonstrated (3)
6:15 Free time
6:45 Supper
7:30 Discussion groups: What do we do that discourages a friendship from continuing or deepening? Describe the different types and forms friendships can take.

8:15 Encourage one another (4)
9:00 Pajama party (we did pedicures and gave foot massages)
11:00 Lights out

Sunday
8:30 Personal devotions (5)
9:00 Worship time (singing/sharing/communion/footwashing) (6)
10:30 Brunch and Award ceremony (7)
11:30 Closing prayer and restate aim
11:40 Pack up
12:30 Departure

Notes:

1. *Devotional #1* - Saturday
   - Write down your personal definition of friendship.
   - In what ways does Jesus show us He is our friend based on John 15:12-17?
   - Write down what you see in these verses that characterize friendship.
   - Which of these characteristics do you need to work on the most?
   - In what ways do you demonstrate friendship to others?
   - For personal evaluation:
     Today I feel that...
     __I have meaningful, quality friendships.
     __I would like to have more significant friendships.
     __I need to learn how to be a better friend.
     __a strong relationship with God and my family is all I need.
   - Spend time in prayer talking to God about how you can do better as a friend.

2. *Session 1: Friendship Defined*
I. What is a friend?
II. Why do we need friends?
III. How can I be a friend?
IV. Biblical examples of friendships.

3. *Session 2: Friendship Demonstrated*
I. Types of friendships (i.e., mentoring, common interests, mutual spiritual growth, redemptive relationship with eventual goal of sharing Christ with an unbeliever)
II. Levels and progressions of friendships
III. Responsibilities in friendships

4. *Encourage one another.* Write a short note of encouragement on a index card to each lady in our group. If your group is too large, divide them into smaller groups. Bind the cards together with a ribbon fed through pre-punched holes in the upper corner of the cards.

5. *Devotional #2* - Sunday
How can we show we are Christ's friend on a daily basis? Look up these verses and jot down actions or attitudes that demonstrate a friendship with Him.
- I John 2:15
- Mark 14:37, 38
- John 15:16
- Psalm 32:5
- Jeremiah 15:16
- Matthew 25:37-40
- Proverbs 3:5, 6
- Psalm 34:1-3
- Romans 1:16

6. *Communion (Lord's Supper):* The beliefs of our congregation allowed for us to do this without a pastor. We began with a scripture reading from one of the gospels where Jesus celebrated Communion with His disciples the night before His crucifixion. Have the group sit in a circle. A time of silent prayer followed to allow each one to prepare their hearts for this celebration by having a time for personal confession. Then each woman served the woman next to her, first the bread and then the cup. She would say to the one she was serving, "Jesus' body was broken for you" or "Jesus' blood was given for you."

Foot washing: Our church does not practice this tradition, so this was a new experience for all of us. To avoid anxiety, we did not tell the ladies of this activity prior to the retreat. Before beginning the foot washing, we explained that the purpose was to show our desire to serve one another in love as Jesus demonstrated to his disciples. We tried to remove any barriers that would prevent participation. One of the reasons for the pedicures Saturday night was to let the ladies "pretty up" their feet so they wouldn't be embarrassed to show them. We also divided the ladies into groups of three, letting them select people with whom they were comfortable. Each group found a private spot and was given a basin and a washcloth for each woman. In turn, each woman washed the feet of one other while the third person in the group read aloud selected verses from John 13, which speaks of Jesus washing the disciple's feet. This also served to make the person whose feet were being washed, and the one doing the washing, not feel like they were being watched, as well as giving the third person something to do so they weren't standing there just watching uncomfortably. There was also quiet instrumental praise music being played in the background so that the individual groups didn't feel like they were being listened to by the others. Everyone agreed afterwards that it was a precious and meaningful experience.

> *I had never before participated in a foot-washing service or ceremony of any kind and was nervous about the whole thing. Seriously, what if my feet smelled? But I summoned up the courage to go with two other ladies to find a quiet spot in the big room. The atmosphere was quiet, reverent, and worshipful. As I sat in the chair to have my feet washed, one lady knelt in front of me and the third lady opened her Bible and began reading. It was an incredibly moving and emotional experience, and I will cherish it forever. Linda Young, retreat participant.*

7. Award ceremony: to come back full circle and conclude with something fun, we created enough categories to give each lady an award. You may have to adapt this if your group is too large. (You could give some of the awards to more than one lady, for example.) The retreat leaders met near the end of the retreat to decide who would receive each award. The first phrase is the category for a particular type of friend and the second is a suggested award. You can think of many more but these are the ones we used:

- Laughs with those who laugh; face lotion (for sore cheeks)
- Weeps with those who weep; box of tissues
- Most cheerful; big Smiley Face sticker or badge
- Most transparent; box of cling wrap
- Greatest encourager; package of note cards
- Puts others first (selfless); chocolate, a treat to enjoy for herself
- Most caring; "Good listener" badge
- Best funny story/joke from activity; joke book
- Most friendly; official "Greeter" badge
- Most contagious laugh; certificate with winner's name written in
- One who "came out of her shell" the most; something with a turtle on it, or turtle candy

- Most relaxed; bath beads
- Most available to serve; clapping hands clapper
- Newest to group; list of the names of ladies present
- First one up in the mornings; "gummy worms" for the "early bird"
- Last one up in the mornings, coffee mug

Resources for teaching sessions: *Friendships of Women* by Dee Brestin, *Traveling Together* by Karla Worley, and *Prayer Partnerships* by Quin Sherrer and Ruthanne Carlock.

CHAPTER 10

Getting out of the Saltshaker

Does the thought of sharing your faith bring sweat to your palms and the shakes to your knees? This retreat provides some practical help, including a close look at how Jesus approached people, along with thought provoking activities.

Aim: to understand the responsibility of being the witnesses God would have us be in our own little part of the world.

Theme verse: *You are the salt of the earth.* Matthew 5:13a

Theme song: (many songs available on this topic)

Sample schedule: (This schedule is for the leaders, the participants don't need as many details. Numbers in parenthesis correspond to notes of explanation.)

Friday
12:00 Meet and load vehicles
12:15 Departure
8:00 Arrive at destination, unload and settle in
9:30 Introduction, explain activity (1)
9:45 Snacks and fellowship

Saturday
8:30 Breakfast available
9:00 Personal devotions; (2)
Take a walk (on the beach, or wherever you are, optional)
10:00 Singing, Session 1: *Learning from Jesus* (3)
11:30 Free time
12:30 Lunch
1:30 Prayer time: (for relationships with unsaved)
2:00 Free time
4:00 Singing, Session 2: *Building Bridges* (4)
6:30 Dinner and free time
8:00 Session 3: *Principles of Sharing our Faith* (5)
10:00 Snacks and fellowship

Sunday
8:30 Optional prayer time
9:00 Personal devotions (6)
10:00 Brunch
11:00 Final thoughts and sharing time
Restate aim: to understand the responsibility of being the witnesses
God would have us be in our own little part of the world.
Salt box "pour" (7)
12:00 Pack up and departure

Notes:

1. *Salt Box Activity:* At the beginning of the retreat each woman was given a container of salt (just as purchased from the store) with her name on it. She was to have it in her possession at all times. Every woman was also given a sheet of smiley face stickers. If a woman was found without her salt box, the other women who observed it were allowed to put a smiley face on her box. The purpose of this activity was to remind us that we are always a witness, in all situations whether we realize it or not, and to remind us that others are watching us.

> *But sanctify Christ as Lord in your hearts, always being ready to make a defense to everyone who asks you to give an account for the hope that is in you, yet with gentleness and reverence. I Peter 3:15*

At the end of the retreat, after our sharing time, each woman took her salt box outside and walked to the water and poured out her salt symbolizing her desire to be salt to the world. (Our lodging was directly on the Gulf of Mexico.)

2. *Personal Devotions #1*
Read these passages and answer the questions: John 2:13-22, 3:1-21, 4:7-26.
- What did Jesus do to arouse curiosity, or do that was unexpected?
- Did he always answer their questions?
- What characteristics do you see in the way he related to the various people?

3. *Session 1: Learning from Jesus*
Jesus was a friend of sinners. John 1:39: Jesus invited them to come and see His life. Study example of Jesus in John 4, Samaritan woman.

4. *Session 2: Building Bridges*
How do I make people curious? What questions can I ask them?
After this session we divided into small groups to role play. The women took turns having the role of the "saved one" who asked questions of the "unsaved one" in order to help develop a relationship, and to practice turning the conversation to spiritual things. The goal was not to share the gospel in this conversation, but just to get to know one another; to "build bridges".

5. *Session 3: Principles of Sharing our Faith*
(The resources listed will be of help in fleshing out these teaching sessions. There are also many other resources on the topic of evangelism.)

6. *Personal Devotions #2*
Read John 1:1-14.
Write down questions, (not the answers), that you could ask a person with whom you were reading this passage. For example, here are some for verse 1:
- Why does John call God "the Word"?
- What is the purpose of a word?
- What do you think God was trying to communicate?
- How does John prove the existence of God?

Continue in the same manner through verse 14. You may only have one or two questions per verse and that is fine.

7. *Salt box "pour"*. Our final activity of the retreat was for each one of us to individually take our salt boxes to the edge of the water, spreading out along the shore line, and pour them into the water as a symbolic act of pouring ourselves out as salt into the world.

Resources used: *Evangelism for the Fainthearted* by Floyd Snyder and *Out of the Saltshaker* by Rebecca Pippert.

Unexpected situation: About half way through the retreat, one of the ladies felt that we were being legalistic or unnecessarily harsh regarding the salt box project. As a leadership team, we met separately to discuss and pray about the situation. Our choice was to abort the project or continue. We all felt that we should continue it; however we did gather the group together to discuss it, garnering responses from the ladies. We explained the purpose and reminded the ladies that there are always people watching us, wherever we are. Thus the need to be on guard to the type of representative we are being for Christ. We continued by stating that we don't have the luxury of taking a day off from being a Christian.

Whether it is in conducting a retreat, a Bible study, or another activity, you will, at some point, experience criticism. This is not just you, nor is it necessarily, an indication that you need to change directions. After taking the opportunity to talk with the individual privately for clarification, the issue may be resolved. If not, take time out to evaluate, pray (alone and with your team) for guidance, and then precede with the confidence that God will lead you aright.

Suggestions: This retreat was held at a beach house about six to seven hours drive, so we left earlier on Friday than we normally would have, and arrived home late Sunday evening. This was a little too far to go for a retreat, in my opinion, and would not recommend this. The larger the group, the harder it is to travel a distance with coordinating gas stops, bathroom stops, and foods stops. If you decide to go a distance, allow more time than if it was just one car traveling. We had the use of a house right on the beach at no cost which is the reason we decided to try it. It was a lovely setting and everyone enjoyed it greatly, but the travel time made it difficult for a weekend retreat.

> At this retreat we had to take the "salt container" with us wherever we went and though some did not like this game/teaching tool, I loved it. It had so many applications, such as, that I needed to be salt and light wherever I was...that others in my small world at work and home were watching me and I needed to be a good example...but most touching was at the end of the retreat we were to walk the beach or wherever and talk alone with God and I remember my "salty tears" coming down my face as I realized how much my Lord and Savior did for me, it was a special time of communion with the Lord. (And I am NOT a beach person. I am more a mountain/lake/woods type of person, but God uses all places/spaces to teach and reach us!). Lori Dorman, retreat participant
>
> Loved the beach house and spreading our "salt on the earth". Michelle Caney, retreat participant.

Under Construction

D oes your house need any remodeling? What about your spiritual house? What kind of choices are you making on a daily
basis to make both of these houses a welcoming place for
Christ to dwell? Would they be characterized as wise or unwise choices?
Join your girlfriends this weekend to wise up!

Aim: to understand that when we make wise daily choices, we prepare our heart and home to glorify Christ.

Theme verse: *The wise woman builds her home but the foolish woman
tears it down with her hands. Prov. 14:1*

Theme song: *Make Me Wise* by Bob Kauflin

Sample schedule: (This schedule is for the leaders, the participants
don't need as many details. Numbers in parenthesis correspond to
notes of explanation.) For Saturday, the notes are interspersed with
the schedule due the amount of notes, making it simpler than going
back and forth from the schedule to the notes.

Friday

7:00 Registration

7:30 Construction-themed games (1)

8:00 *The House that God Built* (2)

8:20 Welcome, opening prayer and theme song (sung as a solo)

8:30 Session 1: *Building Blocks* (3)

Special music: recording of *With All My Heart* by Babbie Mason

Introduce *My Heart, Christ's Home* (MHCH) (Munger, 1974). Read aloud the introduction in the booklet and give an overview of Saturday's activities.

8:45 Craft project: decoupage clear glass plates with "celebration" words/theme

9:30 Free time and snacks

Saturday

8:45 Breakfast

9:20 Singing

9:30 *My Heart, Christ's Home* activities

For each room of the house we did the following, (though not always in the same order):

- read the corresponding section in the booklet,
- read a related devotional from *My Heart Christ's Home through the Year* (Robert Boyd Munger and others, 2004)
- had a discussion question and sometimes a related interactive activity.)

Study: The room where we exercise our minds; think about how we can use it for His glory and consider where our thoughts dwell.

- Read devotional, (Robert Boyd Munger and others, 2004, p. 15) to introduce activity.
- Do a memory game activity.

- From *My Heart, Christ's Home* (MHCH) booklet, read the section entitled *Study*. (Munger, 1974, p. 6)
- Discussion question: Besides the Bible, what books have helped shape your spiritual life?

10:00 *Dining Room/Kitchen*: The room where we satisfy our appetites.

- How do you feel about leftovers? Have ladies share ideas for creative use of leftovers.
- Read the section entitled *Dining Room* from MHCH booklet and from the devotional (Robert Boyd Munger and others, 2004, p. 95).
- Discussion questions: When do we substitute food for God? Can we develop an appetite for God? How?

10:15 Cooking demo (We did a very simple snack demo where the ladies just watched. If doing something more complicated allow more time.)

10:30 Break: eat the snack that was demonstrated in demo.

10:45 *Living Room*: The room used for developing relationships, enjoying fellowship, and spending time with friends.

- Read *Living Room* portion in MHCH booklet. (Munger, 1974)
- Discussion questions: What struggles do you have with your personal devotional time? What have you found to be helpful? What do you do to keep it "fresh"?
- Read the devotional (Robert Boyd Munger and others, 2004, p. 177).

11:15 *Workshop*: In this room, our talents and skills create things of beauty.

- Read the *Workshop* section in MHCH booklet. (Munger, 1974, p. 12)

- Read the devotionals. (Robert Boyd Munger and others, 2004, pp. 182,183)
- Discussion questions: What are the ways you have enjoyed serving the Lord that have brought you joy? What keeps you from using the gifts God has given you?

11:30 Craft project: (continued from evening before)

12:15 Lunch

1:15 _Rec room_: (known as Rumpus room in older version of MHCH.) This room is the place for R&R. For some, that might mean watching a movie, doing something with your hubby, playing a game with your family, or working on a hobby.

- Read from MHCH the section entitled, _Recreation room._ (Munger, 1974, p. 14)
- Read from the devotional book. (Robert Boyd Munger and others, 2004, p. 39)
- Discussion questions: How can we glorify God in our times of recreation? In what areas of your recreational life have you seen God transform you?
- Complete Recreational Enjoyment Inventory (William F. Harley, 1995-2016) (5)

2:00 _Bedroom_: Each one reads to themselves the bedroom section of MHCH. (See resource notes at end of chapter.)

- Read from the devotional book. (Robert Boyd Munger and others, 2004, p. 271)
- Discussion questions: What practical steps can you take this week to guard yourself from impurity? What keeps us from sexual fulfillment in marriage as God intended? If you have divorced or single women in attendance you may want to create a separate group for them.

2:15 _Hall Closet_: A place where things are stored and can be kept hidden from view.

- Read MHCH *Hall Closet* section. (Munger, 1974, p. 16)
- Read devotional. (Robert Boyd Munger and others, 2004, p. 54)
- Discussion questions: Why do we want to keep things hidden from God, even though we know we really can't, and not let Him deal with it? How does discouragement affect your pursuit of holiness? In what areas have you found healing when you have let God expose and clean out those hidden things?

2:30 Tour de Home (6)

4:00 Sharing time

- What room of your "house" is in most need of attention?
- What choices have you made so that you can glorify God in your physical house?
- In your spiritual house?

4:30 Warranty Deed (7)

Play recording of song, *My Heart Your Home* by Christy Nockels

5:00 Celebration (8)

5:30 Close retreat with prayer and restate aim: When we make wise daily choices, we prepare our heart and home to glorify Christ.

Notes:

1. *Construction-themed games:* Have several tables set up for ladies to play these games as ice-breaker games.

- *Cup pyramid game:* 10 identical, medium or large plastic cups are placed mouth side down on a table. Two ladies stand on opposite sides of the table, facing each other. With both of them holding a large rubber band, they stretch the rubber band around a cup and then move the cup into position. The goal is to build a pyramid with four cups on the bottom, three on the next row, two on the third row, and then one on top. You may not touch the cups with your hands. Time the building of the pyramid to determine the fastest builders.

- *Jenga game*: This game can be purchased most places games are sold if you can't find one to borrow. It is a game of blocks stacked row upon row. The goal of the game is to pull out blocks on all levels without the whole tower tumbling.

2. *The House That God Built*, by Jan Petersen (a take-off by author of the children's story: *This is the House that Jack Built*). We used cardboard building blocks labeled and added as each paragraph was read to make a pyramid shape. These were the 20 building blocks as named in *Girls Gone Wise in a World Gone Wild,* the title for each chapter being a "block". For example: Heart, Attitude, Habits, etc. (Kassian, 2010)

The House that God Built

This is the woman who lives in the house that God built.

This is the woman who keeps Christ first in her heart, who lives in the house that God built.

This is the woman who listens to God's counsel above all, who keeps Christ first in her heart, who lives in the house that God built.

This is the woman whose approach is to trust in God, who listens to God's counsel above all, who keeps Christ first in her heart, who lives in the house that God built.

This is the woman whose attitude is gentle and calm, whose approach is to trust in God, who listens to God's counsel above all, who keeps Christ first in her heart, who lives in the house that God built.

This is the woman who shows by her habits a self-disciplined life, whose attitude is gentle and calm, whose approach is to trust in God, who listens to God's counsel above all, who keeps Christ first in her heart, who lives in the house that God built.

This is the woman who lives her life with a godly focus, who shows by her habits a self-disciplined life, whose attitude is gentle and calm, whose approach is to trust in God, who listens to God's counsel above all, who keeps Christ first in her heart, who lives in the house that God built.

This is the woman who has the appearance of beauty, inside and out, who lives her life with a godly focus, who shows by her habits a self-disciplined life, whose attitude is gentle and calm, whose approach is to trust in God, who listens to God's counsel above all, who keeps Christ first in her heart, who lives in the house that God built.

This is the woman who in body language no confusion will breed, who has the appearance of beauty, inside and out, who lives her life with a godly focus, who shows by her habits a self-disciplined life, whose attitude is gentle and calm, whose approach is to trust in God, who listens to God's counsel above all, who keeps Christ first in her heart, who lives in the house that God built.

This is the woman who looks in the Bible her role to read, who in body language no confusion will breed, who has the appearance of beauty, inside and out, who lives her life with a godly focus, who shows by her habits a self-disciplined life, whose attitude is gentle and calm, whose approach is to trust in God, who listens to God's counsel above all, who keeps Christ first in her heart, who lives in the house that God built.

This is the woman who stays sexually pure, no sin to feed, who looks in the Bible her role to read, who in body language no confusion will breed, who has the appearance of beauty, inside and out, who lives her life with a godly focus, who shows by her habits a self-disciplined life, whose attitude is gentle and calm, whose approach is to trust in God, who listens to God's counsel above all, who keeps Christ first in her heart, who lives in the house that God built.

This is the woman who sets boundaries, yes, indeed, who stays sexually pure, no sin to feed, who looks in the Bible her role to read, who in body language no confusion will breed, who has the appearance of beauty, inside and out, who lives her life with a godly focus, who shows by her habits a self-disciplined life, whose attitude is gentle and calm, whose approach is to trust in God, who listens to God's counsel above all, who keeps Christ first in her heart, who lives in the house that God built.

This is the woman who acts authentically in every deed, who sets boundaries, yes, indeed, who stays sexually pure, no sin to feed, who looks in the Bible her role to read, who in body language no confusion will breed, who has the appearance of beauty, inside and out, who lives her life with a godly focus, who shows by her habits a self-disciplined life, whose attitude is gentle and calm, whose approach is to trust in God, who listens to God's counsel above all, who keeps Christ first in her heart, who lives in the house that God built.

This is the woman who shows by her possessions she's not prone to greed, who looks to God for every need, who acts authentically in every deed, who sets boundaries, yes, indeed, who stays sexually pure, no sin to feed, who looks in the Bible her role to read, who in body language no confusion will breed, who has the appearance of beauty, inside and out, who lives her life with a godly focus, who shows by her habits a self-disciplined life, whose attitude is gentle and calm, whose approach is to trust in God, who listens to God's counsel above all, who keeps Christ first in her heart, who lives in the house that God built.

This is the woman who relies on God not to depart, who shows by her possessions she's not prone to greed, who looks to God for every need, who acts authentically in every deed, who sets boundaries, yes, indeed, who stays sexually pure, no sin to feed, who looks in the Bible her role to read, who in body language no confusion will breed, who has the appearance of beauty, inside and out, who lives her life with a godly focus, who shows by her habits a self-disciplined life, whose attitude is gentle and calm, whose approach is to trust in God, who listens to God's counsel above all, who keeps Christ first in her heart, who lives in the house that God built.

This is the woman who speaks graciously as an art, who relies on God not to depart, who shows by her possessions she's not prone to greed, who looks to God for every need, who acts authentically in every deed, who sets boundaries, yes, indeed, who stays sexually pure, no sin to feed, who looks in the Bible her role to read, who in body language no confusion will breed, who has the appearance of beauty, inside and out, who lives her life with a godly focus, who shows by her habits a self-disciplined life, whose attitude is gentle and calm, whose approach is to trust in God, who listens to God's counsel above all, who keeps Christ first in her heart, who lives in the house that God built.

This is the woman who influences rightly at the start, who speaks graciously as an art, who relies on God not to depart, who shows by her possessions she's not prone to greed, who looks to God for every need, who acts authentically in every deed, who sets boundaries, yes, indeed, who stays sexually pure, no sin to feed, who looks in the Bible her role to read, who in body language no confusion will breed, who has the appearance of beauty, inside and out, who lives her life with a godly focus, who shows by her habits a self-disciplined life, whose attitude is gentle and calm, whose approach is to trust in God, who listens to God's counsel above all, who keeps Christ first in her heart, who lives in the house that God built.

This is the woman who sustains relationships by doing her part, who influences rightly from the start, who speaks graciously as an art, who relies on God not to depart, who shows by her possessions she's not prone to greed, who looks to God for every need, who acts authentically in every deed, who sets boundaries, yes, indeed, who stays sexually pure, no sin to feed, who looks in the Bible her role to read, who in body language no confusion will breed, who has the appearance of beauty, inside and out, who lives her life with a godly focus, who shows by her habits a self-disciplined life, whose attitude is gentle and calm, whose approach is to trust in God, who listens to God's counsel above all, who keeps Christ first in her heart, who lives in the house that God built.

This is the woman with a teachable heart, who sustains relationships by doing her part, who influences rightly from the start, who speaks graciously as an art, who relies on God not to depart, who shows by her possessions she's not prone to greed, who looks to God for every need, who acts authentically in every deed, who sets boundaries, yes, indeed, who stays sexually pure, no sin to feed, who looks in the Bible her role to read, who in body language no confusion will breed, who has the appearance of beauty, inside and out, who lives her life with a godly focus, who shows by her habits a self-disciplined life, whose attitude is gentle and calm, whose approach is to trust in God, who listens to God's counsel above all, who keeps Christ first in her heart, who lives in the house that God built.

Note: This ended up being rather long, so if you want to use something like this you might want to think of another way to present it. For example, instead of one narrator, a different woman could read each paragraph. Or add two "bricks" at a time.

3. *Session 1: Building Blocks*

    I. God as the foundation of our "home" (spiritual house) vs. a "home" built with idols (of the heart, based on Isaiah 44:1-23)

    II. Summary of 20 building blocks from *Girls Gone Wise in a World Gone Wild.* (Kassian, 2010)

4. When the *devotional book* is referred to, it is a book called My *Heart-Christ's Home through the Year.* (Robert Boyd Munger and others, 2004)

5. *Recreational Enjoyment Inventory.* Have each lady fill out this questionnaire of recreational activities as a tool to discovering common interests with husband and/or others in their home. It is a very extensive list which likely will reveal some new or fresh ideas not previously thought of, or perhaps, long forgotten. (William F. Harley, 1995-2016)

6. *Tour de Home:* An activity in which each woman rotates through the rooms studied in the activities of the retreat. They can be actual rooms or "mock-up" rooms of a house. The women were asked not to speak to one another during the "tour" so as to allow uninterrupted personal meditation and reflection. (Restrain yourself from rigidity here and allow grace to be the rule.) There were several women in a given room at any one time. Each woman had a study guide and a Bible which she used in each room to look up scripture and answer questions related to the activities that went on in each room as discussed in prior sessions using MHCH, the devotional, and the discussion questions.

Warranty Deed: We used an 8 ½" X 11" sheet of paper folded in half with a graphic on the outside and the deed on the inside. The graphic was a cropped 6 panel door which formed a cross design with a heart shaped knocker in the center. The words for the Warranty Deed read:

Warranty Deed made this _____ day of _____, 20____ by _____ whose address is _____, City of _____, County of _____, State of _____ for the price of the blood of Christ, my Savior, whose address is Heaven, does hereby transfer all of her interest in her own life, together with all her possessions, interests, goals, and spiritual fruit thereof and warrants the title to the same.

_____ (Signature)

8. *Celebration*: This closing activity was to remind ourselves that we glorify God when we celebrate His presence in our lives. A light snack was served in which each lady used her newly decoupaged plate on which to have her food.

Resource Notes:
1. *My Heart - Christ's Home* (MHCH) (Munger, 1974)There are several editions of this booklet. The main differences we found were updated names for the rooms of the house, some additional rooms in the newer versions, and differing text for the bedroom section. Some focused on the bedroom as a place of rest while others focused on moral purity. There were even differences when the focus was on moral purity, one more appropriate for a single person, one more appropriate for a married person. We found the most economical place to purchase these booklets to be through the Billy Graham Evangelistic Association.

2. *Heart - Christ's Home through the Year.* We had difficulty finding this devotional book because it is out of print, but were able to locate copies through used booksellers. (Robert Boyd Munger and others, 2004)

3. We did not use this resource, but there are some skits on YouTube depicting what it would be like if Christ visited our home.

Suggested change: The schedule for this retreat is really too tight. We were trying to do it in a 24 hour period. If it was extended into Sunday, it would be fine, allowing for periods of free time.

CHAPTER 12

What's in a Name
(a mini-retreat)

D o we understand what it is to really worship? How can we deepen our worship? Use this mini-retreat as a way to explore the names of God through interactive activities, music, prayer and teaching which together can lead to meeting Him in Spirit and in truth as true worshipers.

Aim: To understand the truth of Who God is, as revealed through His names, so that our worship of Him will expand and grow deeper.

Theme verse: *Ascribe to the Lord the glory due to His name; Psalm 29:2a*

Theme song: *Worthy of Worship* by Mark Blankenship/Terry W. York

Sample schedule: (This schedule is for the leaders, the participants don't need as many details. Numbers in parenthesis correspond to notes of explanation.)

Saturday
9:00 Registration
9:15 "Name" activities (1)
9:50 Singing
10:00 Skit (2)
10:15 Small group discussion (3)
10:45 Session 1: *Understanding Worship* (4)
11:30 Free time
12:00 Lunch
1:00 Session 2: *Practicing Worship - Part 1* (5)
2:30 Break
3:30 Session 3: *Practicing Worship – Part 2* (6)
5:00 Free time
5:30 Dinner
6:30 Closing worship time (7)

Notes:

1. *Name activities:*

    • *Who am I?* Everyone present has her name on two name-tags, one she wears in the typical way and one that is placed on the back of *another* person. By asking yes and no questions of others, each lady determines whose name is on her back. After asking one question, each lady moves on to ask another lady a question so that she is mingling and talking with many people.

    • *A Special Name:* Have each person share something about their first, middle or last name: i.e., meaning of the name, person for whom they were named, or circumstances around how they were named.

2. *Skit*:

The purpose of the skit is to demonstrate how we sometimes misplace our worship. Elvis is the object of worship by one of the actresses. She describes what sacrifices she has made for tickets to his concert, and in an effusive manner, the character qualities she admires in Elvis, (including different names by which he has been known), and how anything he suggests to his fans, they follow. The other actress makes comments, questioning the degree to which she is going to "worship" another human. The three facets of worship listed below, in the first teaching session, are each brought out in the dialogue.

3. *Small group discussion*: Use with groups of six to eight, each with a designated discussion leader. (Suggestions for leading a discussion group can be found in Chapter 3.)

- How did the skit demonstrate worship?
- How would you define worship?
- What is included in worship?
- When do you know that you have worshiped?
- Based on John 4:21-24, what is necessary for worship to occur?
- What is worshiping **not**?
- What prevents worship? See Psalm 24:3, 4
- What encourages worship?

4. *Session 1: Understanding Worship* (Genesis 22, John 4:21-24)

I. Worship through obedience

II. Worship through sacrifice

III. Worship through acknowledgement of a person's character

IV. Failure to worship

5. *Session 2: Practicing Worship* (Part 1)

Using God's names give us a:

I. Venue for meditation, (a place to park our mind)

    A. Brainstorm: As a group, make a list of God's names or attributes.

    B. Share: Encourage ladies to select one of the names listed and tell why it is meaningful or precious to then.

    C. Discuss:

- What facet of God does each of these names (or attributes) demonstrate?
- What are the implications of each name?
- Example: *Provider.* Everything I have comes from God, which implies that He is the source of all that I need, and He is the one I need to go to because no one else can meet my every need at the right time and in the right way.

II. Vehicle for praise, (a way to transport us into praise)

- Examples of David: Psalms 3 and 46. David enumerates names and attributes of God to provide expressions of praise in prayer.

6. Session 3: *Practicing Worship* (Part 2)

Using God's names gives us a:

III. Voice for petitions,

- Match a need to a corresponding name upon which to call.
- Example: when you need help in a stressful relationship experiencing conflict, call on the Prince of Peace, Counselor, Judge, and the God of love, grace and humility.

IV. Victory in spiritual warfare, (weapons to fight the battle)

- See Psalm 18:3, Proverbs 18:10.
- Stand strong and firm as you remember these applicable names, using them as weapons in prayer: Almighty, Victor, Strength, Refuge, Deliverer, Sovereign, Fortress, Salvation, and Lord of Hosts

So what's in a name?

- Endless meditations
- Infinite praises
- Powerful petitions
- Victorious warfare

7. *Closing worship time*: sing, share, and pray

- Sing songs of praise that enumerate names and attributes of God.
- Provide an opportunity for the ladies to share what God had shown them throughout the day.
- Group prayer: Encourage the ladies to kneel to pray, if they are able. After a brief explanation of the pattern for prayer, the leader begins each of the three segments. These are sentence prayers offered randomly and multiple times, if desired.

1. Praise: A time to exalt God for who He is, reciting His names and attributes
Examples: "Lord, You are faithful." "Lord, You are the Sovereign God and there is nothing that happens to us that is outside of your control."

2. *Thanksgiving*: Offer thanks for specific blessings, ways God has been seen at work.

Example: "Thank you, Father, for Your Word which I can freely read where I choose and in a language I can understand."

3. *Petition*: Praying for one another based on requests written out beforehand on cards and passed out for those who are willing to pray aloud for that specific need.

- Responsive reading: *Who is a God like Ours?* (Gunter, 1991)

- Closing song: *How Great is Our God?* by Chris Tomlin

- Restate aim: Today we have explored the truth of Who God is, as revealed through His names, so that our worship of Him will expand and grow deeper. May God enable us in this endeavor.

- Prayer

CHAPTER 13

Touching Ladies with Prayer

D o you have the longing and desire to touch others through the prayers you offer and feel burdened that you should pray for them while at the same time wonder if your prayers really make any difference? During this retreat we will learn how those prayers really count.

Aim: To realize God makes our prayer for others powerful and effective.

Theme verse: *The prayer of a righteous man is powerful and effective.* James 5:16b NIV

Theme song: *Teach Me to Pray*, (see note #4)

Sample schedule: (This schedule is for the leaders, the participants don't need as many details. Numbers in parenthesis correspond to notes of explanation.)

Friday
6:00 Registration
6:30Dinner
7:30 Welcome and introduction
7:45 Show and Tell (1)
8:30 Skit (2)
8:50 Story time (3)
9:00 Theme song and closing prayer (4)
9:15 Free time/snacks

Saturday
8:30 Singing/Session 1: *Prayer Power Tools* (5)
9:15 Personal time
10:30 Brunch
11:30 Small group discussion 1: *God's Power and Sovereignty* (6)
12:15 Singing (songs related to God's power and sovereignty)
12:30 Session 2: *Understanding God's Power and Sovereignty* (7)
1:00 Prayers of praise and thanksgiving (8)
1:30 Free time/snacks
2:30 Small group activity (9)
3:15 Small group discussion 2: *Biblical Examples of Prayer* (10)
4:00 Prayer notebook project (11)
5:00 Free time
5:30 Supper
6:30 Talk Show: *Powerful Examples from the Bible* (12)
7:30 Prayers of intercession (13)
8:00 Closing: sharing, song and prayer (14)

Notes

1. *Show and Tell*: Have each lady share about an effective or powerful product, tool or gadget they have found useful in any area of life. (It

is helpful to have them know about this activity prior to the retreat so they have time to think about it and bring something to show, if applicable.)

2. *Skit*: To present struggles that can keep us from powerful and effective prayer. (We had little vignettes depicting the various topics. End with silent prayers as each woman examines her own heart.) The following questions provided the framework for the skit. What is keeping me from powerful and effective prayer?

- Being unsure that I'm praying with right words?
- Not believing that God will do what He says He will do?
- Seeking my own agenda instead of His?
- An independent spirit that thinks I can handle things on my own?
- Not understanding the blessing of prayer?
- Depending on others to carry the responsibility of prayer?
- Being unwilling to spend the time or effort?
- Indifferent to needs of which God makes me aware?

Lord, teach me to pray.

3. *Story Time*: Stories of effective and powerful prayers. Use a combination of personal examples from predetermined individuals as well as selected stories read by various individuals from *Voices of the Faithful*. (Kim P. Davis, 2009) or another source. Besides reading several Friday evening, we read a couple at each meal.

4. *Theme song*:
Teach Me to Pray (lyrics by Jan Petersen, sung to the tune of *Freely, Freely* by Carol Owens, verse only, no chorus)

Teach Me to Pray

There is pow'r in the prayer of the righteous one,
It's because we pray through God's own Son.
There is great effect and power in prayer
For those weighed down with sin and care.

Oh- Lord teach me, teach me to pray,
This is my heart cry day to day.
I long to know Your will, Your way,
Te-ach me to pray, teach me to pray.

5. *Teaching session 1: Prayer Power Tools*
In this session talk through the worksheet step by step to prepare the ladies to work through it alone during their personal prayer time. (The ideal situation is for each woman to have a designated, fairly private place for her to go through this worksheet.) The comments or questions given by the leader are printed in *italics* below and are NOT included on the worksheets the ladies receive. The non-italicized words are printed on their handout for them to read and answer on their own.

Personal Prayer Time: suggested worksheet
Quiet yourself before God, ask Him to remove distractions, and reveal Himself to you.

Praise your Lord and King. Worship His majesty.

This section focuses on who God is. Look up the verses listed and write what you learn about who God is. The first two are done for you as examples. Continue this pattern with other passages.

For personal study: What do you learn about God from these verses?

- Isaiah 6:3: He is holy; He is the Lord Almighty
- Romans 11:33: His wisdom and knowledge are unfathomable.
- Psalms 100
- John 14:6

How has God shown you His character this week?

Come to your Lord and King with a grateful heart. Thank Him.

(Follow the same pattern in this section as the prior one. This one is focused on thanksgiving.)

For group discussion: *Why are praise and thanksgiving powerful prayer tools? (Ask for responses before giving input.)*

- *it puts our focus on Him instead of our problems*
- *as we are reminded of who God is, it strengthens our faith in bringing Him requests*
- *they are expressions of our love for Him*
- *we realize anew our need of Him*

For personal study: What do you learn about giving thanks from these verses?

- Psalm 30:11-12: He takes the hard and hurtful things in my life and turns them into something for me to sing about.
- 2 Corinthians 9:15: He gave me the indescribable gift of His Son, Jesus, and salvation
- Psalm 9:1
- 1 Thessalonians 5:18

List what God had done for you this week for which you are grateful.

Come to your Lord and King with a clean heart. Confess your sin.

For group discussion: *What makes confession a powerful prayer tool?*

- *It humbles us and God promises to give grace to the humble,*
- *He resists the proud*
- *It removes the barrier in our fellowship with Him that sin brings*

For personal study:

What do you learn about confession from these verses?

- Hebrews 8:12: He forgives my wickedness and He doesn't remember my sin – *ever.*
- Romans 8:1: He doesn't condemn me.
- Psalm 139:23-24
- 1 John 1:7-9

Confess ways you sinned this past week.

Come to your Lord and King on behalf of others and yourself.

This last section focuses on intercessory prayer..

For group discussion: *"4 Power Tools to Utilize in Making Requests":*

A: Ask God who and what He wants you to pray for today, (don't be tied to or limited by a list).

B: Believe He will answer: Hebrews 11:6

C: Continue to ask: for scripture on persistence read Matthew 7:7 (Verb tense used means keep on asking, keep on seeking, and keep on knocking.)

D Do battle: remember who we are in Christ, use our shield of faith to deflect the lies of Satan, and wield the sword by praying Scripture. (See Ephesians 6:10-18).

For personal study: What do these verses tell you about intercession?

- Isaiah 59:16a: God was appalled that there was no one to intervene on behalf of others.
- I Timothy 2:1-4: It pleases God when I intercede for others, including for those in authority.
- Ephesians 6:10-18
- Romans 8:26

Who do you feel burdened to pray for most right now? A family member or relative, a friend, a political leader, an unsaved person, a co-worker...

What requests will you pray on their behalf?

6. *Small group discussion 1: God's Power and Sovereignty*

Have the women divided into groups of six to nine prior to the time for discussion. (Chapter 3 gives suggestions on leading a small group.) These discussion questions are to "prime the pump" for the teaching to follow on this topic. This is the handout for each member of the group to have for the discussion.

God's Power and Sovereignty: Discussion Questions

These questions are for small group discussion to prepare for the teaching session. Answers do not need to be written down. Discuss as many questions as possible in the allotted time. If you do not finish them all, that is okay.

- What kinds of things have you seen God do in your life this week?
- Have you prayed for something so long that you thought it would never happen? What?
- Do you easily give up praying or continue to pray when nothing seems to change?

- What does it mean to say God is sovereign?
- Since God is sovereign and His purpose will prevail, why do we need to pray?

Read the account of a violent storm recorded in Acts 27:13-44. When God revealed that He would deliver Paul and all his shipmates, Paul trusted God and His promise of deliverance. Even so, Paul didn't passively sit expecting God to do the work that the sailors were equipped to do.

- Name all of the actions that were taken that helped fulfill God's promise that they would all reach land safely.
- How does this account show the relationship between God's sovereignty and our responsibility?
- Do you think there are ever times when our responsibility might be to do nothing? Why?

7. Teaching session 2: God's Power and Sovereignty
Overview: Powerful and effective prayer is possible only because God is sovereign and powerful. This gives the basis for and moves us to pray.
Introduction: (Illustration using a vacuum cleaner for a prop). Let's pretend each of us is a vacuum cleaner. According to the manufacturer (and the salesman), we are perfect. The owner's manual touts all the wonders we can do: besides the regular uses, we can pick up spilled rice, scattered cat food, even runaway marbles. We can clean refrigerator coils, pull out the air from specialty vacuum seal bags, and with the special attachments reach cobwebs from the ceiling, suction coins from between couch cushions, and retrieve toys from the bowels of furnace vents. But no matter how many features and special attachments this vacuum cleaner has, there is a secret to its power and effectiveness. (Point to an electrical outlet.) It is the

power source. And when we plug into our power source, we can confidently tackle any cleaning job there is. Our power source is not subject to overloads on the grid, wind, ice storms, or interruptions due to construction. Therefore, we could say that cleaning with the perfect vacuum cleaner is powerful and effective. Powerful and effective prayer is possible ONLY because God is sovereign and powerful. This gives the basis for and impetus for us to pray. The phrase, "hand of God", is used 190 times in the Bible in reference to God's power and authority. The Greek word "dunatos," related to "dunamis," means ability, abundance, capability, mighty works, miraculous power, and prevailing strength. It is the root of our English word "dynamite."

I. God's Hand

Just what does the Bible say His power can accomplish, which in turn, impacts our prayers for others? *(Notice reference in verses to God's hand.)*

A. His hand brings us out of bondage.

> *You shall remember that you were a slave in the land of Egypt, and the Lord your God brought you out of there by a mighty hand and by an outstretched arm; therefore the Lord your God commanded you to observe the sabbath day. Deuteronomy 5:15*

1. Give an illustration of someone who has been freed from bondage in a particular area.
2. Application questions:
- Do you pray that God will bring His children out of the bond of slavery to a particular sin?
- Do you believe He can do that? How does it show?
- For whom can you pray that God will bring out of bondage?

B. His hand refines.

Pity me, pity me, O you my friends, for the hand of God has struck me! Job 19:21.

1. Review life of Job along with this verse.

2. Give an illustration of a "refining experience."

We can pray for God's mercy for those who are being refined by the Lord. We can pray for acceptance of and softened heart to respond to God's refining process, for ourselves and others.

C. His hand convicts of sin.

For day and night your hand was heavy upon me; my vitality was drained away as with the fever heat of summer. Selah. I acknowledged my sin to You, and my iniquity I did not hide; I said, "I will confess my transgressions to the Lord," and You forgave the guilt of my sin. Selah. Psalm 32:4, 5

1. Give an illustration of a time when God convicted you of a sin in your life.

2. Application question:

• Do you have a burden for someone living in open, blatant sin?

It is God's job to convict, not ours. We can pray for their eyes to be opened to the sin and for a responsive heart evidenced by confession, repentance, and acceptance of His forgiveness.

D. His hand creates both physical life and spiritual life.

In whose hand is the life of every living thing and the breath of all mankind? Job 12:10

1. Physical life: Remember that life and death is in His hands as we pray for those facing life and death issues, struggling with infertility, or who are trying to challenge God's authori-

ty in that area. Give an illustration of God's obvious hand in a situation of birth or death.

2. Spiritual life:

No one can come to Me unless the Father who sent Me draws him, and I will raise him up on the last day. John 6:44

Give an illustration of a time when God created spiritual life. Pray for God to create spiritual life where there is no life. It is easy to think someone is "too hard" or "too far gone" to ever come to Christ for salvation.

3. Application question:

• For whom are you praying for God to create new life in Christ?

E. His hand displays His greatness and might.

Moses said "O Lord God, You have begun to show Your servant Your greatness and Your mighty hand; for what god is there in heaven or on earth who can do such works and mighty acts as Yours? Deuteronomy 3:24

That all the peoples of the earth may know that the hand of the Lord is mighty, so that you may fear the Lord your God forever. Joshua 4:24

1. Give an illustration of God's mighty power being displayed.

No prayer request is beyond His ability to answer. Situations that seem impossible, have hit a dead end, or problems with no visible solution can be resolved by Him.

2. Application questions:

• Do you know someone facing an "impossible" situation?
• How are you praying for them?
• Can you think of any need which His power cannot meet?

Let's return to the vacuum cleaner illustration. If I had the #1 rated vacuum cleaner, let's call it *Miele Sovereign* after the highly rated German made Miele vacuum cleaner, you would expect it to be a powerful machine. Sovereign implies powerful.

> *God's sovereignty is the attribute by which He rules His entire creation, and to be sovereign, God must be all-knowing, all-powerful, and absolutely free .* (Tozer, 1961, p. 108)

We could also define sovereign as having supreme rank, power, and authority.

II. Over what is God Sovereign?

A. Nature: Examples of Paul and the shipwreck, Jonah and the big fish.

B. Nations: Seen in the Minor Prophets as they speak of God using various nations to bring judgment on Israel.

C. People:

> *The king's heart is like channels of water in the hand of the LORD; He turns it wherever He wishes. Proverbs 21:1*

D. Circumstances:

> *And we know that God causes all things to work together for good to those who love God, to those who are called according to His purpose. Romans 8:28*

We see the tension involved as God's sovereignty does not remove our responsibility to act prudently. Jerry Bridges explains how the two go hand in hand.

> *To act prudently, in this context, means to use all legitimate, biblical means at our disposal to avoid harm to ourselves or others and to bring about what we believe to be the right course of events. One of the most basic means of*

prudence that God has given to us is prayer. We must not only pray for His overruling providence in our lives, but we must also pray for wisdom to rightly understand our circumstances and use the means He has given us. (Bridges, Trusting God, 1988, p. 108)

When we pray we acknowledge God's sovereignty, and when we act prudently we acknowledge the responsibility He gives us. Another verse that illustrates this tension is Psalm 127:1:

Unless the Lord builds the house, they labor in vain who build it; unless the Lord guards the city, the watchman keeps awake in vain.

God's responsibility is stated along with ours.

Understanding God's power and sovereignty affects our prayer life. We can trust Him with anything and everything. It is the reason our prayers are ever powerful and effective.

(We closed this session with a vocal solo of *On My Knees* by Jaci Valasquez.)

8. *Prayers of praise and thanksgiving*: Since this is a prayer retreat, there are a number of opportunities for prayer with different types of prayer suggested for each one. This one is designated for the whole group to offer sentence prayers of praise, which acknowledging who God is, and thanksgiving, which acknowledges what God has done.

- Examples of praise: *You are a forgiving God, removing our sins as far as the east is from the west. You are powerful. There is no other God like You.*
- Examples of thanksgiving: *Thank you for your forgiveness when I blew it again with my son last night. Thank you for showing me your power by arranging the circumstances...*

If your group is larger than 20 you may want to split them up into smaller groups. (Specific prayer requests are shared at the intercessory prayer time later.)

9. Small group activity: Each group (comprised of the same members as the earlier discussion group) creates their own skit/commercial/song on the topic of intercessory prayer, lasting one to two minutes. (Intercessory prayer refers to those prayers given on behalf of someone else.) Any number of means can be used to communicate an aspect of this topic:

- create a short skit,
- write your own words to a familiar folk song like: *Row, Row, Row your Boat*
- select a well-known commercial and adapt it
- draw a series of pictures
- do a pantomime.

Have every member of the group participate in some way. Each group then performs for the others.

10. *Small group discussion #2: Powerful Examples from the Bible*
Using the same discussion groups as previously,

- read the assigned example of intercession from scripture
- answer the related questions
- be prepared to share with the whole group in a talk show format. Designate a spokesperson in each group who will join the talk show hostess.

Suggested passages: John 17:6-12, II Kings 6:8-18, Exodus 32:1-13, Colossians 1:1-14 (Each group studies a different passage.)

1. Who was praying?
2. For whom was he praying?

3. What was the situation that moved him to pray?

4. What was/were the request(s) made?

5. What was the desired outcome or outcomes of the intercessor?

6. What lessons do you learn from this intercessor?

11. *Prayer notebook project*:

Begin by explaining each section of the notebook while you show the sample. Then, let the ladies make their own notebooks, guided by written instructions as laid out below. This particular format was inspired by looking at a variety of samples shown on YouTube. It is a tool that God can use in helping to develop a more intimate relationship with Him through prayer.

PRAYER NOTEBOOK:

This is *your* notebook, modify these directions as desired. They are just guidelines to get you started. A prayer notebook can transform you prayer life, but only if it is used. It is a tool to guide you into delight, not a slave to drive you into duty.

Supplies needed: binder, nine tab dividers, paper, paper clips, and index cards. (We used the half size binder which holds 5 ½" X 8 ½" paper and has the clear overlay to insert a cover sheet. This size notebook seems easier to work with.)

Directions:

1. Make cover insert: If you get a clear view binder, you can design your own insert for the cover or use a graphic from the Internet.

2. Label tabs with these headings and insert into binder: (Adhesive tabs on cardstock can be substituted as an economical alternative.)

- Praise
- Confession
- Thanksgiving
- Requests (this one is for daily requests)
- Sunday, Mon-Tues, Wed-Thur, Fri-Sat, (we used one tab for two days except on Sunday)
- Listening

3. Insert tab dividers into binder in the order listed.

4. On the back side of each divider, paper-clip the corresponding index card on which you have written the following notes for that particular category. They are:

PRAISE: Praise God for who He is
- based on scripture you have just read
- using the names and attributes of God list (There are enough for a different one each day of the month.)
- singing or reading songs and hymns
- reading selected Psalms

Names of God

Father	Lord and Master
Bread of Life	Bridegroom
Creator	Defender/Protector
Deliverer	Fortress/Refuge
Good Shepherd	High Priest
Healer	Helper
Immanuel	Judge
King of Kings	Lamb of God
Light	Prince of Peace
Provider	Redeemer
Resurrection and the Life	Savior

Strength	Truth
Victor	Way
Wonderful Counselor	Advocate
Friend	Guide
Living Water	

Attributes of God

All-knowing	All-powerful
Comforting	Compassionate
All-sufficient	Ever-present
Faithful	Forgiving
Gentle	Gracious
Holy	Infinite
Loving	Longsuffering
Majestic	Merciful
Patient	Sovereign
Steadfast	Just
Sustainer	Trustworthy
Understanding	Worthy
Wise	Available
Kind	Generous
Eternal	Good
Refining fire	

CONFESSION:

- promptings from the Holy Spirit through sermons, Bible studies or your Bible reading
- wrong thoughts, words, actions, attitudes
- times I've ignored God's prompting
- times I've yanked back control in certain areas of my life

THANKSGIVING: for what God has done

- answers to prayer
- daily gifts of grace
- evidence of God's timing and/or intervention

REQUESTS:

- Write "Daily" on one index card and write names of those for whom you wish to pray daily. Clip to back of the "Requests" tab divider.
- On the back of the first page in each section of the day of the week, make a list of whom you will pray for that particular day. This will be the left page of the two facing pages. If your tab is for two days, make 2 columns of names, one list for one day and another list for another day. (Both columns will be on the left half of two facing pages.) On the right page of the two facing pages, put any specific requests you may have for the people you listed.
- If you have a prayer partner, you may want to use an additional tab divider specific for the requests that the two of you share.

LISTENING: What God has taught me through:

- reading the Bible
- sermons
- Bible studies or books
- life experiences
- prayer

5. Insert paper in each section.

6. Punch holes in any handouts you may wish to add, such as the one with the names and attributes of God, which would be appropriate in the "Praise" section.

Suggestion: You may want to put a notepad in the front pocket of your notebook to jot down any random thoughts that come to you during your prayer time so you can attend to them later, thus preventing distractions from sidetracking your prayer time.

12. *Talk Show*: *Powerful Examples from the Bible*
This is an opportunity for each small group to give the insights in a talk show format. The talk show host asks each spokesman to share what their group learned from the discussion questions. An option is to follow this with a short teaching using Abraham's example as an intercessor in the story of Sodom and Gomorrah (Genesis 18:16-33). The outline we used is provided here.

When God places a burden on our heart for someone, it is a call to intercede.

I. Awareness of the Need: Genesis 18:16-21
We can't pray for the whole world, but we can pray for those whom God burdens our heart.
Application questions:
- For whom has God burdened my heart today?
- What am I doing about it?
- For what purpose does God reveal needs to me?
- How often do I wait and listen to God so that He can reveal those for whom He wants me to intercede?
- When I learn of a need do I respond with indifference or intercession?

Because we are friends of God, He reveals needs to us for which He wants us to intercede.

II. Praying for the Need: Genesis 18:22-32
Abraham acknowledged who God is. Abraham didn't demand a particular outcome. He persisted in prayer and was specific in his request. Though Abraham asked God questions, he did so respectfully.

When interceding on behalf of someone, we should pray boldly, specifically, and respectfully.

Application questions:
- What attitude do I have when speaking with God?
- Do I intercede on the basis of what I know His character to be? Why or why not?
- How persistent am I in praying?
- Do I pray specifically or in vague generalities?

III. Relinquishment of the Need: Genesis 18:33
When Abraham finished interceding, he returned home. In my opinion, this demonstrates submission and relinquishment of the burden to God's will. Because he was at peace, he was able to leave and go home.

After interceding we need to leave the burden in God's hands and go in peace.

Application questions:

- Do you give the burden to God and then "pick it up" again, or do you know the peace that comes by leaving it in His hands?
- What need do you keep "picking up" that you need to leave in His hands today?

When God places a burden on our heart for someone, it is a call to intercede.

13. *Prayers of Intercession*: Earlier in the day the ladies had an opportunity to write a prayer request on an index card for something God had put on their heart, whether for someone else or themselves. Having the requests written out beforehand allows for a better use of the time than sharing each request verbally. As the cards are passed around, those who are comfortable praying aloud can select one. Then, one at a time, each need is prayed for. One suggested format is for a woman who selected a card to read the request aloud, allow time (maybe 30 seconds) for everyone to pray for that request silently, and then she briefly prays for that need aloud. The next person repeats the sequence: read request, allow for silent prayer, and pray audibly. (You may want to make sure everyone understands the plan.) Depending on the size of the group you may need to make some adjustments.

14. *Closing*:
- Sharing: What has God taught you about prayer in our time together? It could be something from your personal prayer time, from the teaching sessions, from the discussions, or from the skit.
- (After the sharing, each lady was given the pamphlet entitled, "The Lord's Prayer" produced by Rose Publishing.)

- Restatement of Aim: As God teaches us to pray He makes our prayers for others powerful and effective.
- Close with the theme song and prayer.

Conclusion

For those of you who are considering being involved in planning a retreat, it is a spiritual work you desire. What can you expect? Expect to see God work on your behalf, in big ways and in small ways. Because He is the Creator, He can give you creative ideas. Because He is our Provider, He can meet every need. Because He is Powerful, He can handle obstacles. Look for His hand through it all. Expect to confront obstacles and face spiritual warfare. Expect to work hard. And yes, expect to experience blessings in abundance as you undertake a ministry with great potential for impact among the ladies who attend. It is a work that can be done in human strength and abilities, but the result will not be a work of the Spirit. Or it is a work that can be done with the Lord's strength and power, with the result of hearts challenged and lives changed. You may not see the fruit of your efforts in this life, but, the harvest will come. Remember the words of Paul

> *Let us not lose heart in doing good, for in due time we will reap if we do not grow weary. Galatians 6:9*

The stresses in women's lives threaten to pull them apart. You have the opportunity and privilege to provide a time and place for them to *come apart* before they come a-p-a-r-t.

ALSO AVAILABLE:

Companion **ORGANIZER** for:

Come Apart before

You Come A-P-A-R-T

This helpful eBook contains **20** individual worksheets in PDF format as a companion to the retreat guide. It will help you keep all your notes organized as you plan your retreat.

Sample worksheets:

Important Dates
Volunteer Assignments
Facility Notes
Publicity Plans
Expense Worksheet
Activity Plans

Order at: comeapart2retreat.wix.com/Petersen

Notes

Bibliography

Batterson, M. (2012). *Praying Circles around Your Children.* Grand Rapids, Michigan: Zondervan.

Bridges, J. (2007). *Respectable Sins.* Colorado Springs: Navpress.

Bridges, J. (1983). *The Practice of Godliness.* Colorado Springs: Navpress.

Bridges, J. (1988). *Trusting God.* Colorado Springs: Navpress.

Elliot, E. (1982). *Discipline: The Glad Surrrender.* Grand Rapids: Revell.

Gunter, S. (1991). *Prayer Portions.* Birmingham: The Father's Business.

Kassian, M. (2010). *Girls GOne Wise in a World Gone Wild.* Chicago: Moody.

Kim P. Davis, B. M. (2009). *Voices of the Faithful, Book 2.* Nashville: Thomas Nelson.

Munger, R. B. (1974). *My Heart Christ's Home.* Downer's Grove: Inter-Varsity Christian Fellowship.

Robert Boyd Munger and others. (2004). *My Heart-Christ's Home through the Year.* Downer's Grove: InterVarsity Press.

Tozer, A. W. (1961). *The Knowledge of the Holy.* New York: Harper Collins.

William F. Harley, J. (1995-2016). *Marriage Builders Forms and Questionnaires.* Retrieved from marriagebuilders.com: http://www.marriagebuilders.com

69139361R00082

Made in the USA
Middletown, DE
05 April 2018